MW01172881

Early Praise for The Headache Advantage

My praise for The Headache Advantage

If our prime purpose in this life is to help others, then Dr. Scott Vrzal has not only succeeded at that immensely for himself but has given this book as a gift for others to achieve this noble pursuit with a clear path to freeing them from the pain and suffering that headaches bring. We have all had friends and loved ones who have lost hours and days of life to headaches, and to make clear to them that those days can be permanently in the past, is conferring one of the greatest benefits to humankind.

Beyond being a must-read for anyone affected by headaches whether as a patient, caregiver or healthcare professional, The Headache Advantage stands out for its emphasis on patient empowerment, shifting the paradigm to understand symptoms as messengers to guide one to a higher quality of life and health, not just something to be stopped or avoided. Thoughtfully structured, Dr. Vrzal's approach is particularly refreshing and inspiring as it guides the reader through his effective management strategies. I will be keeping copies of this book in my clinic library for all those who need what this book brings (and takes away) from their lives in order to live life to its fullest.

Dustin Strong is the founder and chief clinician of Strong on Health as well as a featured practitioner author, speaker, educator and product innovator. Mansfield, TX

Even with over a decade of experience in natural health care and having treated thousands of patients, I continue to learn from Dr. Vrzal. I use his approach in practice daily, because it works! It is a privilege to call him both a friend and colleague, and an even greater honor to have been trained by him, both as a student and as a patient. I wish my parents had access to this book during my youth, as I suffered from chronic "incurable" headaches for many years. The valuable insights in this book will benefit both practitioners and patients, alike. These teachings, seldom covered in formal education, highlight Dr. Vrzal's exceptional expertise and clinical acumen. By sharing this information, he is answering God's calling and generously imparting his knowledge to all who are willing to learn.

Thank you, my friend!

-Ryan Zernonis, DC, ACN, CCWFN. Louisville, KY

An amazing road map to help those who are suffering chronic and stubborn headaches. Dr. Vrzal has done a great service to humanity that gets directly to the root cause of this horrible pattern of pain. I have successfully used Dr Vrzal's methodology to help many patients get well and stay well. What a blessing to those who have searched high and low for a solution!

Dr. Andre Camelli, Founder of Life Quest Wellness Center, International Speaker, and bestselling author of "Cracking the Code; Unlock Your Genetic Potential." Cortland, OH

The content explores the connection between headache location and underlying health issues in various organs, glands, or hormones. It emphasizes that headaches are not mysterious but can serve as indicators of bodily imbalances. Great book which is extremely informative and helpful. No more headaches as easy as 1-2-3!

Steven E. Schmitt Co-Founder of Wakeupocevent. com, Bestsellerguru.com Book: How I Sold Millions of Books. San Diego, CA

Understanding our body may seem straightforward, yet it operates as a remarkably intricate machine that facilitates our life experiences. Dr. Vrzal clarifies the understanding that our body communicates with us, signaling with headaches or other pain to alert us that something is amiss. He delves deeply into this concept, offering practical advice on how to interpret and internalize these signals. Dr. Vrzal's work highlights the importance of seeing ourselves as whole beings—body, mind, and soul—and understanding what our bodies are telling us. His ability to simplify complex medical information makes his insights accessible and actionable, empowering readers to take a proactive approach to their health and well-being.

Edgar Reynoso Vanderhorst MD Author of Wellness: Optimizing Yourself: A Scientific Perspective from a Pediatric Neonatologist. Chicago, Illinois

"In a healthcare world of over specialization, Dr. Vrzal is in an elite group of doctors that understands how the organs and body communicate with each other. Pain or dysfunction in one aspect of the body in a particular location doesn't necessarily mean that's where the problem is.

This is perfectly illustrated in his book, The Headache Advantage.

This isn't just a book for patients. It's a book for doctors."

Dr. David Vaught. Louisville, KY

Wow! Dr. Vrzal makes it simple to demystify headaches and find solutions to gain relief. When modern medicine lacks to find answers for many, this book helps to reveal that your symptoms are actually the path to the cure! This is absolute gold for anyone that suffers from headaches or practitioners that work with headache sufferers.

Dr. Michelle Green-Vagner. Erie, CO

Dr Vrzal offers a groundbreaking perspective on headaches, connecting them to various organs and body systems. This book provides a holistic approach to headache relief, combining expert insights on chiropractic care, whole food supplements, and lifestyle modifications. An essential read for anyone looking for comprehensive and natural solutions to headache management.

Lee Carroll BSc, BHSc (WHM) MNHAA, medical herbalist/educator, Brisbane, Queensland, Australia

True story: One hot October evening in the mid-60s my good friend Bob and I were sitting in my front yard underneath our huge magnolia tree. Bob turned and asked me, "What do your headaches feel like"? I told him I did not know what he was talking about because I had never had a headache in all my life. He was amazed. I asked him why he asked such a question. He said he thought everyone had headaches. His dad had headaches, his mom had headaches, and his two brothers had headaches. He never knew someone without headaches. He asked how I avoided them. I told him I had been regularly seeing a chiropractor since I was born.

The brain proper has no pain fibers. A doctor could poke around all day long in your head and not cause you pain. The pain signals come from other sources, which Dr. Vrzal explains. If you want to get a handle on your headache pain look no further than, *The Headache Advantage; 7 Pain Patterns as Tools for Total Body Transformation.*

Michael D. Allen, DC, NMD, Functional Neurologist, Author: *What Your Brain Might Say if It Could Speak,* and, *Receptor Based Solutions; Functional Neurology Every Doctor Should Know* President: Allen Chiropractic, PC Founder: HealthBuilderS® Professional Coaching

"Dr Vrzal may have just cracked the code on a common health issue that's as old as time, Headaches. The Headache Advantage demystifies an often-debilitating problem that affects millions worldwide giving the reader, probably for the first time ever, a distinction as well as real time solutions for their specific type of headache. A must read for headache sufferers and clinicians alike"

Dr Howard Cohn Founder, Cohn Health Institute and The Bio Stacking Summit

THE HEADACHE ADVANTAGE

7 Pain Patterns as Tools for Total Body Transformation

Dr. Scott Vrzal

ISBN: 979-8-89316-679-8 - Paperback
ISBN: 979-8-89316-660-6 - Hardcover
ISBN: 979-8-89316-678-1 - eBook

The mere fact that you are holding this book in your hand demonstrates that you are motivated to make a change. You will learn that:

Pain is intended to elicit *change*.
The potential solutions for the 7 patterns of head pain.
You are designed to THRIVE.

The advantage of pain in the head is that it can
direct you to where your body needs help.

If you would like to jump start success, go to
www.HeadacheAdvantage.com.
You will find easy to implement trigger food lists.
You can easily order supplements tailored to your headache pattern.
There are also videos of other self-care protocols.

Go to www.HeadacheAdvantage.com
to start feeling better today

CONTENTS

Forward...xi
Introduction: Heads Up: My Story Is Your Cure xv
Quiz: Test Your Headache IQ... xxvii

PART I
THE HOW OF HEADACHES

Chapter 1   WHAT'S IN A HEADACHE?....................................3
             Your Canary in a Coal Mine 3

Chapter 2   THE SCIENCE OF PAIN 16
             The Surprising How of Hurt 16

Chapter 3   SMOKING GUNS TO ANY KIND OF
             HEADACHE.. 26
             Dietary, Environmental, and Emotional Triggers 26

PART II
UNLOCKING YOUR HEAD'S UNIQUE PAIN

Chapter 4   LEFT-SIDED HEADACHES 45
             Problem in the Stomach.................................... 45

Chapter 5   RIGHT-SIDED HEADACHES 54
             Problem in the Gallbladder 54

Chapter 6   BACK-HEAD PAIN ("TENSION HEADACHES")....65
             Problem in the Thyroid 65

Chapter 7   FRONTAL (FOREHEAD) HEADACHES................. 75
             Problem with Stomach Lining 75

Chapter 8   CYCLOPS HEADACHES 86
             Problem in the Pituitary Gland 86

Chapter 9   PAIN IN THE SIDES OF THE HEAD (TEMPLES)....92
             Problem with Hormone Balance 92

Chapter 10 PAIN THAT SURROUNDS THE HEAD
             ("HEADBAND PAIN")... 100
             Problem in the Large Intestine 100

PART III
ENDING YOUR PAIN WITH THE H.E.A.D. PROGRAM

Chapter 11 HEAL THE MAIN TRIGGER/WEAKNESS 113
             Solutions to the Common Culprits 113

Chapter 12 EDIT YOUR DIET AND ENVIRONMENT........... 142
             Eat Wisely, Factor in Your Blood Type, and
             Minimize Exposures... 142

Chapter 13 ALLOW FOR SLEEP, EXERCISE, AND
             STRESS REDUCTION... 161
             How to Find Balance in Life 161

Chapter 14 DEDICATE (AND TROUBLESHOOT).................. 176
             Q&A 176

Notes 185
Acknowledgments... 197
Index 201

FORWARD

*Prepare To Be Enlightened, Empowered,
and Ultimately, Pain-Free.*

When I had the pleasure of hosting Dr. Scott Vrzal on Episode 523 of The Learn True Health Podcast with Ashley James, titled "Headache Decryption: Understanding Your Headache or Migraine Pain Location To Decode Root Cause Holistic Solutions," he made the complex world of tracking down the root causes of headaches straightforward and delightfully clear. His insights were profound and presented in a way that made holistic health solutions accessible and actionable for everyone.

Dr. Scott Vrzal's book "The Headache Advantage" is a groundbreaking exploration into the often-misunderstood world of headaches. This book isn't just about managing pain; it's about transforming your life by understanding the underlying causes of your headaches. Millions of people that suffer from headaches are sick and tired of the drug-based approach which offers them harmful short term Band-Aid options instead of supporting the body's ability to heal itself through uncovering and addressing the root cause naturally. This book will inspire and motivate you to take control of your health and transform your life.

Dr. Vrzal reveals that "your headaches—and exactly where you experience the hurt—are clues to problems elsewhere in the body, and they manifest as pain in the head" (p. 6). With his extensive experience and deep understanding, Dr. Vrzal provides a clear roadmap to resolving headaches at their root. The drug-based way only gives us negative side effects, whereas Dr. Vrzal's book "The Headache Advantage" provides the positive side effects of enhancing your overall health and vitality.

Dr. Vrzal's approach is both revolutionary and refreshingly straightforward. He states, "Virtually all head pain will fall into one of these seven distinct patterns. That's it. Seven" (p. 7), emphasizing the simplicity and efficacy of his method. This book is a must-read for anyone seeking to reclaim their health and live a life free from the debilitating effects of headaches. You can be confident that Dr. Vrzal's method will guide you to a pain-free life, reassured by its simplicity and effectiveness.

To Your Health!

---Ashley James, *Learn True Health* podcast, Author of
Addicted to Wellness
Integrative Health Coach, Author, Podcaster,
Anxiety Cessation Expert

*For the tens of thousands of souls who have trusted me
for direction in their pursuit of vibrant health. I have
learned from each and every encounter, thank you.*

*It is truly profound how transformative small changes can
be in one's quality of life, which then empower everyone else
around you. May the information contained herein provide
a distinct **advantage** in the vitality of you and yours.*

A wise man should consider that health is the greatest of human blessings, and learn how by his own thought to derive benefit from his illnesses.

~ Hippocrates

INTRODUCTION

Heads Up: My Story Is Your Cure

"Where does it hurt?"

It's the question we all get at some point. Our answers help healthcare professionals know where to pay attention to attempt to address and correct an issue. But not all pain springs from where the pain is felt, and this is especially true when it comes to headaches. That's right: your headaches—and exactly where you experience the hurt—are clues to problems *elsewhere* in the body, and they manifest as pain in the head. Let me cut to the chase.

Left-sided headaches are likely caused by a problem in the stomach. Right-sided headaches are often triggered by a problem in the gallbladder or with bile movement. Pain in the center of the forehead can be caused by an imbalance in the pituitary gland. Too much chronic stress that disrupts your gut function and a breakdown of the stomach lining can lead to frontal headaches. Back-of-the-head pain, commonly called tension headaches, are commonly due to thyroid imbalance. Pain emanating from the sides of the head can happen when the hormones are out of whack. Head pain that surrounds the head like a headband occurs when the large intestine is not functioning properly. Virtually all head pain will fall into one of these seven distinct patterns. That's it. *Seven*.

Now, that might sound a little absurd if this information is new to you, but you're about to embark on a journey to understand what I mean and learn how you can heal yourself quickly and, dare I say, painlessly. It will take effort, but it will be worth the slight shifts in your daily habits to achieve the results you crave. These counterintuitive associations between the specific location of the head pain, various organs, glands, or hormones have been scientifically documented for more than thirty years and backed by thousands of years of evidence from ancient medicine.

Recent technologies employed in research circles have only bolstered the library of data. As a practicing doctor who has used this knowledge to relieve thousands of patients, the time has come to share this wisdom with the world. I can only reach so many people in my private practice, yet I feel everyone deserves a fighting chance to end their pain. So, fasten your seatbelt!

The title of this book probably surprised you. How could headaches provide an advantage? As my patients will tell you, I like to say there's a *benefit* to headaches. Your headaches are canaries in the coal mine and can inform you about abnormalities in your biology that are often easy to fix without drugs or expensive regimens. They can teach you how to elevate your health using basic lifestyle strategies to fix those issues in the body. They are your compass to finding optimal wellness and, ultimately, freedom from pain.

It's precisely why this book is titled *The Headache Advantage*. Once you understand the significance of your headaches' location and learn how to address them based on their "geography," you can put yourself in the proverbial driver's seat of your health and attain what you want from your body and so much more. After all, don't we all want a body that we know how to take care of and that loves us back? Don't we all want to feel vibrant and hopeful about the future? Without your health, nothing else really matters.

If you're skeptical about my approach, read on. I have yet to see a patient fail my protocols, and as we journey through this revolutionary method, you'll find plenty of resources couched in scientific citations. I have gone to great lengths to support my statements and suggestions, knowing that I am bringing forth a new perspective and presenting ideas counter to the conventional wisdom of the day. Contrary to popular perception, headaches are not poorly understood and difficult to manage. They are not a mystery to me, and I wouldn't have written this book if I were not confident in my message and practical lessons. Headaches are baffling to just about everyone, leaving most feeling like the solution is not understood. But they are, unfortunately, all around us. Someone within a mile or two of you right now is likely harboring a pounding headache. Perhaps you are too.

Headaches are among the most common disorders in the world. Up to three-quarters of adults have had at least one in the past year, with one in twenty adults suffering from a headache every, or nearly every, day. And children are not immune: more than half of school-age kids get them, and a skyrocketing 80 percent of adolescents are afflicted by them. Headaches are, well, a headache. They are costly in so many ways—physically, emotionally, socially, financially, and more. They lower quality of life, disrupt our ability to engage with others and be productive, infuse us with anxiety and fear of the next one, and basically leave us disabled and suffering.

Most people, when struck with one, reach for a potential Band-Aid remedy like aspirin, ibuprofen, or acetaminophen and hope for the best. Some people rely on prescription medication that comes with potent side effects, particularly those who develop migraines and are told the only way to treat and prevent them is with strong pharmaceuticals. Others believe it's okay to live with chronic headaches because they are just a part of life. After all, everyone has one occasionally, right? Wrong!

Headaches are not a normal part of life, and you shouldn't have to suffer, nor accept the fact you're supposed to have one occasionally. Routinely dealing with headaches and resorting to medications will only exacerbate the problem and prolong the pain.

Studies show that around half of all patients with chronic headaches, migraines included, overuse their medications to the point that short-term drugs—acetaminophen, nonsteroidal anti-inflammatory drugs, triptans, barbiturates, and opioids— trigger new types of headaches. So-called "medication overuse headaches" are the third most frequent type of headache, according to a collection of studies that led to a bold statement delivered at the 17th European Headache Congress in Barcelona in 2023.[1]

The phenomenon is a big reason why people can easily go from experiencing episodic headaches to having chronic headaches with no end in sight. Tapering from the medication and dealing with withdrawal symptoms then becomes another hurdle to clear in seeking sustainable relief.

When you perform an online search using the keyword "headache," you'll soon find yourself reading about the various kinds, and you might begin to think you have a brain tumor or other catastrophic problems. Fear not. The vast majority of headache sufferers do not have a serious, life-threatening malady, and it doesn't matter what you call your headaches, whether they are migraines or not. What does matter is the pain pattern and how that pattern matches with other weaknesses in the body. Fix the weakness, heal the pain. It's as simple as that.

Ultimately, this book is about empowering you to feel—and be—better. Our cars are wired to tell us when a tire's pressure is low or the engine is malfunctioning. When these warning lights come on, we take the vehicle to the mechanic, who plugs it into a computer to retrieve a diagnostic code locating and describing the source of the problem. The information tells the mechanic what to change for the fix. How much more intelligent is our body? Pain is our body's warning light. *"Let pain be your guide,"* as the old adage goes. Technology may someday allow us to "plug in" to a supercomputer that reveals what is compromising our health. But until then, we must rely on clues naturally given to us. The good news is that with the knowledge you gain in this book, you can identify and potentially correct what is compromising your health and fueling your headaches. My bet is the source of your pain is also affecting other aspects of your health equation, such as sleep, weight management, mood, levels of anxiety, stress, and overall energy. Headaches can ruin a lot. Even our relationships are impacted.

Nearly all health concerns emanate from choices we've made or exposures we've had in the hours, days, and years leading up to the pain. When we can identify the cause, it is easier and more motivating to make the correction. For example, the most common cause I see in gallbladder congestion, which sparks right-sided headaches, is glyphosate, a popular herbicide (weed killer) used in conventional farming and found on many non-organic grains (more on this later). The empowering part is knowing and acknowledging the cost of consuming such grains that cause the pain (as an aside, and as we'll explore later on, glyphosate has also been declared a carcinogen, so you're increasing your risk for cancer too when routinely exposed).[2]

I find that when people understand the effects of particular dietary choices, they are far more likely to make better decisions. These simple changes then drastically improve the quality of life and can save thousands of dollars in medical bills and lost productivity. What changes would you be willing to make if it meant more quality time with loved ones, more fruitful work time, less illness (no headaches!), and fewer medical expenses? Even if you apply just a few of my ideas to your daily habits, I trust you'll experience vast improvements in many areas of your life, from your confidence and self-esteem to how you relate with others and take on the world.

MY STORY MAY BE RELEVANT TO YOURS

My health journey began when I was twelve years old while watching my beloved grandfather slowly, painfully die. I used to enjoy fishing and watching lightning storms on the porch with Grandpa Kenny. My fond memories of him got overshadowed by the final two years of his short life when he battled cancer and arthritis. He left my grandmother as a widow for her surviving forty-two years.

About a year after watching Grandpa Kenny finish his life suffering deeply when I was thirteen, I unexpectedly passed out at a public event. There was no obvious reason for me to faint like that, and it alarmed my parents. Fortunately, on the referral of a family friend, my parents took me to a holistic health practitioner. I underwent a six-hour glucose tolerance test and allergy testing that determined I was allergic to wheat and had hypoglycemia (low blood sugar). At the time, I was typically eating the biggest donut I could get at the local Winchell's donut shop. I was the class clown, regularly in peril and unfocused at school. The doctor told me that if I did not change, I would eventually develop diabetes and need to give myself daily shots of insulin. I didn't take his advice seriously until...

A week later, I was playing racquetball and found myself quitting halfway through the game. My body could not keep going for the ball. My mom asked, "What did you eat?" I replied, "A donut, of course."

I quit eating sugar that day. I got the message.

Then, in junior college, I developed debilitating headaches whenever I worked out, especially after doing bench presses. These headaches would encase my head and throb harder and longer when I pushed myself. I couldn't leave the gym after a session without a pounding headache. I tried rest and anti-inflammatory medications to no avail. This time my concerned parents took me to a traditional doctor who ordered a CAT scan with contrast, wondering if I might have an aneurysm. Lo and behold, the CAT scan showed no abnormality! At that point, I was told to go see a psychiatrist.

This happens more than you realize: When exhaustive tests on patients turn up nothing unusual, doctors will then think there's an underlying psychological problem—that it's "all in their head." Such a "diagnosis" did not sit well with me. By the grace of God, when the headaches returned with a vengeance one year later, I shared my story with a gym partner who happened to be a chiropractic intern at the time.

"Not sure we can help, but let's give it a try," he told me, then we proceeded to have him perform an adjustment on me. It was like magic, and it was the beginning of my crusade.

Driving home in my little faded yellow Volkswagen Bug, I had the most incredible free feeling in my head, and I wanted to feel like that for the rest of my life. More importantly, I wanted those I loved to also experience such bliss. I recalled the test I had taken to gauge my personal interests toward a career. My highest score pointed me to the field of chiropractic, which made sense because I was a natural bodybuilder who was already obsessive about diet and healthy lifestyles. A career in chiropractic offered the perfect opportunity for me to help others as well as feel my best. My newfound passion and purpose made school a lot more exciting. I was now all in, and I was no longer going to be a class clown.

By the time I was in chiropractic college, I made it my mission to learn from the most effective doctors. I was responsible for bringing many of the top names in healthcare to the campus for presentations. I quickly decided that the doctors who seemed to have the tools to figure out or fix virtually any condition had *one thing* in common: They all used the late, great Dr. George Goodheart's applied kinesiology (AK). I spent many weekends attending kinesiology seminars, enough to accumulate 300 hours of AK during my formal chiropractic training. This accomplishment allowed me to be a teaching aid for the next decade with Dr. Robert Blaich's fine 100-hour AK courses. During those years, I also took the 100-hour course with the late, wonderful Dr. Wally Schmitt. Both were preeminent educators in the field.

I am so incredibly thankful for the amazing platform those years created for this voracious information gatherer. That was the season when I learned the revelational concept of muscle-organ-nutrition correlations. This benefits us in that we can now understand what the pain is warning us about. Don't panic if this seems abstract; we'll be taking baby steps so you can fully grasp the important takeaways. All I ask of you is that you have an open mind and be willing to challenge old beliefs about headaches and medicine in general. Make room for a totally new perspective. Only then can you open yourself up to new possibilities—and a headache-free life.

Here is what's key to know: Every area of pain is a sign of what is wrong inside. Those signs are easy to read when you know where to look. Pain is a prompt to take action! Pain motivates. Pain teaches. Pain is intended to inspire change. Act on it. Don't just suppress the pain. Listen to what your body is trying to tell you. It's speaking to you, and I'm going give you the tools to decipher its message. Then you can learn from the pain.

With the strong desire to prevent others from going through the "care" I received for my headaches, I quickly got busy identifying the pain patterns of any headache I encountered in my practice. Confident that every pain was a warning for internal turmoil, I employed the tools I had learned in applied kinesiology to identify the cause. It quickly became obvious that there are only seven different types of headaches. I hit a stride in my practice as I began to eliminate a headache before a patient would leave the office. And better yet, the patient would know what the root cause was and make the appropriate modifications to avoid future headaches. Thus, the Vrzal Technique was born. And my practice exploded largely through word of mouth alone.

7 Head Pain Patterns:

1. *Right side*
2. *Left side*
3. *Across the front of the head*
4. *At the back of the head*
5. *In both temples*
6. *Around the whole head*
7. *In the "third eye" area*

Each will be discussed with its associated causes.

Of course, the solutions have progressed dramatically and been refined since 1993, when I first figured out the patterns. But the patterns have remained the same and been proven over and over again by tens of thousands of happy patients. For me, the most amazing fact is that I can count the number of headaches on one hand that did not go away during treatment. That statement is not meant to toot my own horn—it's to tell you that these methods work, and these pain patterns are real.

I share these numbers to build your confidence in understanding and resolving your headaches. The answer is out there. And if you are looking for relief from headaches, chances are fairly good that you are currently holding the roadmap to it in these pages. Although I won't be able to perform any typical chiropractic adjustments on you through this book, I've designed this program to be just as powerful and effective, and it can work in tandem with any other lifestyle program or healthcare regimen you follow. In fact, correcting a single nutritional "miss" can eliminate the need for a physical adjustment.

I've divided this book into three parts, beginning with a quiz (coming up shortly) to test your ingrained knowledge about headaches. In Part I, "The How of Headaches," I'll give you a general overview of headaches with a new spin that shows my tried-and-true philosophy in treating them. I'll be going into depth about the surprising behavior of pain and the connection between headaches and specific organs, grounding the conversation in the scientific literature to date. Some of this literature will reference centuries-old traditions in Chinese medicine, with a focus on acupuncture meridians. I'll also cover the smoking guns to any kind of headache that almost everyone encounters in daily life today (*spoiler alert: you'll want to put down that energy bar and diet soda*). Then, in Part II, "Unlocking Your Head's Unique Pain," I'll explain the seven pain patterns and begin to divulge how you can address the root cause of your pain.

Finally, in Part III, "Ending Your Pain with the H.E.A.D. Program," you'll follow a step-by-step protocol that you can tailor not only to your type of headache but to your personal preferences and lifestyle. This program is not about unrealistic, rigid rules. My whole goal is to make this doable, practical, fun, and enjoyable without extreme measures (or even a commitment to piles of supplements). Peppered throughout the book are true stories from my own case files—proof of transformed lives. Even though the program is saved for Part III, you'll encounter strategies throughout the book as you read, and I'll give you plenty of options to consider so you can personalize. I've boxed material and key concepts that I think should be highlighted and reinforced from the main text. Don't forget to check out my website at HeadacheAdvantage.com for additional resources and an active list of recommended brands for products I suggest to enhance your success.

My hunch is you've picked up this book for a reason. You or someone you love is in pain, and you've tried everything else. I'm thrilled that you're here. And I wish you a speedy recovery—for life. Prepare to be surprised, engrossed, and eventually healed. My hope is for you and those around you to achieve a top quality of life and to be forever improved. Earlier I said that we all deserve a fighting chance to be headache-free. To that I'll add, we all deserve the most vibrant life free of disease and disability for as long as possible. We must earn that achievement through how we live. And this is an excellent place to start. *Where does it hurt?*

Let's take advantage of your pain...and uplevel everything about you.

Test Your Headache IQ

How much do you know about headaches? Find out using the following true/false quiz. Don't think too much about each statement; answer as best you can (you're not being scored). The answers are on page 18 . By the end of the book, you'll have a full understanding about these topics and will be able to come back and ace the test.

1. Headaches are largely genetic, so if they run in your family, you're doomed.
2. Headaches are among the top causes of disability worldwide.
3. Headaches are primarily the result of the brain's pain sensors going haywire.
4. Migraines are distinct from headaches; migraines cannot be cured and require special attention and medications to prevent and/or resolve.
5. Caffeine can both trigger and alleviate headaches.
6. Sugar causes headaches.
7. Sinus headaches are typically caused by allergies or infection.
8. Only women can have frequent headaches.

9. Over-the-counter drugs are the best go-to for regular headaches.
10. Stress alone cannot trigger headaches.
11. There's a high chance that chronic headaches are caused by a tumor or aneurysm.
12. The majority of people with chronic headaches have food sensitivities.
13. There is a close association between high blood pressure and headaches.
14. Dehydration is the most common cause of headaches.
15. Mood conditions and anxiety disorders are common among chronic headache sufferers.
16. The quality of your drinking water can cause headaches.
17. Zinc deficiencies are widespread in the population and an undercurrent to headaches.
18. Dysfunction in the stomach or other parts of the digestive system are not thought to trigger headaches.
19. Acid-reflux medications can predispose one to headaches, not to mention autoimmune conditions.
20. Low-fat diets can help prevent headaches.
21. The popular weed killer glyphosate (Roundup) does not pose a risk to humans as long as it is used according to directions.

Answers:

1.	False	8.	False	15.	True
2.	True	9.	False	16.	True
3.	False	10.	False	17.	True
4.	False	11.	False	18.	False
5.	True	12.	False	19.	True
6.	True	13.	False	20.	False
7.	False	14.	False	21.	False

PART I

THE HOW OF HEADACHES

CHAPTER 1

WHAT'S IN A HEADACHE?

Your Canary in a Coal Mine

When was the last time you had a headache? Last week? Yesterday? If you have one at this very moment, for how long has it been speaking to you? Can you understand its message?

You will soon. And yes, your headache is trying to tell you something important. Something that can transform your life and wellbeing. There's a surprising benefit to that pain.

I have not had a headache since the 1990s. I know, it sounds unrealistic, but you too can be headache-free for life. Think about what life can be like without another headache. It would be the ultimate game changer, right? It would impact everything about you—your productivity at work, your resilience against stress, your relationships (especially your most intimate ones), your behaviors, your sleep quality, your energy levels and motivation to exercise, your ability to take care of and show up for others, your patience, your self-confidence, your mood, your attitude, your overall sense of self, your happiness, your quality of life...and so on.

Really take a minute or two to envision being pain-free. How much younger would you feel and look? How much money could you save on medical expenses? How much more could you accomplish? How much longer could you extend the length of a healthy, better life? I bet it is a lot. To be headache-free is to be completely available to engage in life to its fullest.

Too many people have come to accept headaches as a fact of life and somehow learn to live with them. After all, we call any disruptive nuisance that we have to deal with a "headache." The secondary, informal definition of the word *headache* is "a thing or person that causes worry or trouble." Headaches are indeed a hassle, inconvenience, pain, and *pest*. We act as if they are inevitable, unavoidable, and allowable. Why? When your check-engine light comes on in your car, do you cover it up with a piece of tape so you can't see the warning sign? Do you reflexively change the oil even though the problem has nothing to do with that?

No, of course not. You do what smart car owners do—you contact a qualified mechanic right away before the problem worsens, get it diagnosed precisely, and then fix the error. It boggles my mind that more than half of the world's population is impacted by headache disorders, yet there's no rallying cry to end the shared misery. This is a public health crisis! I rejected that mindset decades ago and enjoy a pain-free life. Unlike other common conditions that are endemic and associated with age, such as cancer, dementia, and cardiovascular disease, headaches are universal across all ages. I can't believe we never hear much talk about combating them amid all the health-related headlines incessantly in the news. Talk about ending obesity, diabetes, cancer, and Alzheimer's disease, among other top health challenges, is constant. But talk about ending headaches?

> *Headache research is poorly funded, yet headaches are our most common form of pain. They are a major reason for missed work and school, as well as trips to the doctor. They are also the leading cause of disability in people under the age of fifty.*[1]

Even more than typical body pain, headaches cause one to become very irritable, unfocused, distracted, and quite often simply unable to do basic tasks. Even more alarming is the fact that the pain is trying to warn the sufferer of a greater impending problem looming. For example, is the head pain an alarm for gallbladder, thyroid, stomach, or intestinal problems?

What also astonishes me is how the medical community barely acknowledges the gravity of this epidemic. A shocking comparison: In 2023, the National Institutes of Health—the largest public funder of biomedical research worldwide—spent only about $56 million on headache research while doling out more than four times that amount, or roughly $232 million, on epilepsy research.[2] All this investment, yet headaches are twelve times more common than epilepsy. Not until 2023 did a small study—albeit the first of its kind—emerge that aimed to "provide an in-depth understanding of how chronic headache adversely affects the lives of sufferers."[3] The researchers sought to answer a simple question: "What is life like with a chronic headache?" Not surprisingly, the study led to some stunning admissions among participants, patients between the ages of 38 and 68 who were visiting an outpatient clinic in Norway. Among the emotions expressed about their chronic headaches were shame, anger, sadness, and even loneliness.

Here are some of the responses to describe how their headaches impacted them:

- *I'm often angry and I swear a lot. I didn't use to. Everything annoys me. Little things that don't mean anything. I become easily overwhelmed, sometimes I cry, not because I'm sad, but because I'm angry. Even in front of my kids, I can explode.*
- *I feel judged…like they look down on me. I am embarrassed and don't know why. It's like I am an addict! I go to different pharmacies so that I don't meet the same shop assistants.*
- *I feel sad—numb, completely numb, like a zombie. I don't think about getting better; I just try to make it through the next hour.*
- *I lost myself, somewhere. My identity—gone, washed away by pain and illness. I don't know how to find myself again.*
- *I miss having freedom in my life. Everything needs to be kept under control—to be predictable.*

I know, it's hard to read and think about all that suffering. The researchers concluded that the healthcare systems in society (even wealthy ones) underestimate the complexity of chronic headaches and more attention needs to go toward improving treatment at the individual level. To that I say, *hear hear!* But first, there needs to be a greater collective understanding about how to treat—and prevent—headaches, and as you might expect, I have a few things to say about that.

CAUSE VS. TRIGGER

When you go online to research common causes of headaches, migraines included, you'll encounter a lengthy list of ideas: hormonal fluctuations, poor sleep, poor posture, pet dander, pollen, mold, fumes from chemicals or fragrances, food allergies or sensitivities, infection, chemical exposures, disrupted circadian rhythm, changes in the weather and air pressure, stress and other emotions, lack of exercise, genetics, nutrient deficiencies, low blood sugar, alcohol, medications, eye problems, dental or jaw issues, trauma, sensitivity to light or sound or odors, muscular tension, overexertion, neuroinflammation, hunger, caffeine withdrawal, dehydration, depression, anxiety, secondhand smoke, sensitive brain cells...the list *goes on.*

All of these potential culprits can indeed contribute to and exacerbate a headache, but they may not necessarily point to the root cause of the problem. Many of these reflect collateral damage from certain organs, glands, and tissues not operating well, or they contribute to dysfunctions in the body that have many downstream effects, headaches being one of them. And there's a difference between a *trigger* and a *cause.*

Hormonal changes, stress, and dehydration can trigger the brain to activate painful responses, but they may not be the root cause of the problem. And it can be hard to avoid all potential triggers. The goal should be to get to the root cause and turn off the triggers. Treat the cause, eliminate the triggers. Note also that I include migraines within the larger headache category. Many people, doctors included, often place migraines in a separate class—a condition all on its own as if it were a totally disparate disease. Whether it's your ordinary run-of-the-mill "tension-type" headache or a pulsating migraine with an aura, both encompass pain in the head and can be attributed to one of the major pain patterns.

> *The goal is to eliminate the triggers and treat the root cause of the headache, which is likely not in your head.*

Suffice to say, it's a complicated picture, which is why it can be so hard to treat headaches when you focus primarily on the symptoms and play whack-a-mole with remedies. Unfortunately, we live in a world dominated by treatment modalities that ignore the holy grail of all: *prevention*. With all the hyped discourse these days about longevity, better living, and improving health span, you'd think modern medicine would focus more on prevention. But it continues to revolve around treating symptoms, and usually long after a disease has staked its claim in the body. It's much harder and more costly to treat disease than to prevent it. We don't know how to easily treat late-stage lung cancer, for example, but we do know how to largely prevent the ailment altogether: by not smoking. The same goes for type 2 diabetes: It's no picnic to manage raging diabetes with chronic insulin pumping, but it's relatively easy to maintain a healthy diet and keep your blood sugar balanced so you never develop the disease.

Somehow we've come to accept being reactive rather than proactive. We deal with problems as they emerge when we'd do well to thwart the problems entirely, or at least delay the onset of certain conditions. The goal is to live as long as possible without disability or disease—without chronic anything, headaches *included*. Let's surrender to identifying those underlying causes of the pain. Only then can we truly live long and pain-free. In the words of the late Desmond Tutu, "There comes a point where we need to stop just pulling people out of the river. We need to go upstream and find out why they're falling in."

Time to go upstream.

EAST MEETS WEST

Modern medicine is marvelous by many measures, despite its flaws and disproportionate attention to managing disease. We can transplant vital organs (except brains!), stop many communicable diseases that were once leading killers, cure several otherwise debilitating diseases (including forms of cancer), and give people the proven keys to living as long as possible without disability. But we're not living better as we age. On average around the world, we live up to 20 percent of our lives in an unhealthy state. Only 12.2 percent of us, or one in eight Americans, is achieving optimal metabolic health.[4] More than 11 percent of Americans live with diabetes, a number unheard of decades ago. More than 90 percent of those diabetics have type 2, largely driven by lifestyle factors and often reversible through lifestyle habits.[5] Nearly six out of ten Americans have at least one chronic illness, and the number of people with at least three is expected to more than double from 40 million to 85 million by 2030.[6] A whopping 10 percent of the U.S. population now has one autoimmune disease, and the number is growing.[7]

I see this daily in my practice—sick patients desperate for relief from their pain. A great majority of them come to me with chronic conditions other than their headaches: diabetes, allergies, arthritis, asthma, gout, heart disease, kidney disease, thyroid issues, eczema, psoriasis, you name it. These comorbidities undoubtedly play into their headaches too, both metaphorically and physically. My goal is not only to help them figure out the root cause of their pain but to also address that trigger directly with the hopes they can ease some of these conditions and scale back their reliance on drugs over time.

It's amazing to me how simple some of my patients' solutions can be—a single dietary edit like the removal of tomatoes, a rebalancing of stomach acid levels without drugs, or a flushing out of the gallbladder by consuming healthy fats. Several years ago, my mother-in-law had pounding whole-head headaches every weekend starting on Friday evening. My wife was constantly asking her what she was doing differently on weekends to stir the trouble. Finally, they realized that her regular habit was to start Friday night and go through the weekend regularly consuming an instant noodle product. The spice pack contained high amounts of MSG (monosodium glutamate), a problematic ingredient used as a flavor enhancer that has a neurotoxic component (see Chapter 3). Once she nixed this habit, my mother-in-law's headaches significantly lessened to occasional right-sided headaches. For those, we started her on a supplement that naturally supports the gallbladder, and she has been headache-free for more than twenty years. You'll be delightfully surprised to learn how easy the solutions are to get to the bottom of your chronic pain. And to fully grasp the connection between, say, the state of your gallbladder and right-sided headaches, it helps to have a lesson in biology, one that's thousands of years in the making.

You've probably heard about Eastern or traditional Chinese medicine. Broadly speaking, Eastern medicine refers to a system of medical practices that originated throughout Asia, notably China and India, centuries ago. Unlike traditional Western medicine, which is also grounded in ancient philosophy—most notably Greek (think Hippocrates)—but revolves around treating symptoms, as I mentioned, the Eastern approach aims to treat the whole individual rather than just the symptoms. A foundation of Eastern medicine is the appreciation that the whole body is connected through various energy channels—invisible "meridians." The balance of energy and the flow of our life force, called *qi* (pronounced "chi"), through these meridians is what determines whether you are well or unwell. How that *qi* flows through the body along those meridians is analogous to the way nerves and vessels carry messages and blood throughout every system. In fact, there's a lot of interplay between the meridians and our body's physical systems, including its tissues and cellular matrices, that manifests in pain signals.

> *The body is a complex network of superhighways similar to the country's integrated network of road and highways. The body's system of highways ultimately transports the things it needs to survive, from blood and other substances to nerve transmissions, nutrients, biochemical messages, and more.*

Much in the way your circulatory system is a superhighway of blood, your meridians are a superhighway of energy. Every muscle has an associated organ or gland through a meridian. The kidneys are associated with the lower back muscles; the small intestine or stomach is associated with the abdominal muscles and quadriceps. You cannot see these meridians on a scan or X-ray like you can see nerves and blood vessels, but you can certainly see their effects, akin to watching the invisible wind impact the environment and physical structures. According to Dr. Chris Motley, a teacher and practitioner of Chinese medicine, meridian pathways are like maps, and the maps are small lines—microtubules—that make their way through the body's fascia, which is the sheath of thin, fibrous connective tissue that wraps around and supports every structure in your body.[8] Fascia is comprised of proteins, sugar molecules, and water, but it's very electrically conductive. And it's the meridians through the fascia that transmit electrical signals from one organ to the next, helping with blood flow, lymph flow, and so on.

It's important to understand that both Eastern and Western medicine can coexist and complement one another. Although Western medicine has long pooh-poohed Eastern medicine, there's been a tectonic shift in thinking over the past decade. No longer is

Eastern medicine downplayed, rejected, or relegated to the quack department. Much on the contrary, it has earned its place on the playing field, and many of our most respected institutions, from the World Health Organization to the National Institutes of Health, the Mayo Clinic, and academic medical centers affiliated with universities, medical schools, and teaching hospitals acknowledge its importance and devote research dollars to its study. Even Medicare now covers some alternative therapies based on Eastern practices due to the mounting evidence of their effectiveness.

EASTERN MEDICINE CAN HELP US UNDERSTAND REFERRED PAIN CAUSES

While it's intuitive to think the body is interconnected, it's not so intuitive to see how one organ or gland can be so influential to another tissue far away and part of a totally different system. But that's precisely where those meridians come into play. Another way of grasping this phenomenon is to think of the pain experienced during a heart attack. Often, the very first sign is pain felt in the jaw, teeth, neck, or shoulders, even though the problem is not there. This is called *referred pain,* and it happens because the nerves in your body are all connected. Indeed, those energy meridians are similar to what Western medicine calls *neural pathways*.

When a stimulus of pain strikes your body, your nervous system carries the signal to your brain, which then communicates to you that you're experiencing pain. And for the record, the brain has no pain receptors, so it cannot feel or perceive pain itself. In other words, headaches are not the result of pain in the brain. Statement #3 on the quiz is false. Neurosurgeons can operate on a brain with the patient awake. Hence, headaches don't originate from the brain itself. Pain receptors called nociceptors in the brain's surroundings, however, including the meninges (the brain's covering), blood vessels, nerve tissues, and neck muscle can certainly send pain signals when stimulated. These nociceptors send signals through nerve fibers to the brain's nerve cells telling them that part of the body hurts.

> When you experience pain in one area of the body but the pain-causing injury is somewhere else, that's called referred pain. According to the Cleveland Clinic, referred pain "happens because all the nerves in your body are part of a huge connected network."[9] A common example is the experience of eating something cold and experiencing brain freeze—the extreme cold hits your mouth and throat, but you feel the intense shot of pain in the front part of your head.

Sometimes the brain misinterprets the messages and sends a pain signal to a different part of your body than where you actually feel the pain. The complexity of how nerves are wired and how they converge throughout the body also add to the nuances of this phenomenon. Another simple way to make sense of this connection is to consider the experience of feeling nervous, anxious, or embarrassed to the point you have "butterflies in your stomach." Now, you know that's not the case, but the sensation is real, and so is the sensation of sudden heat on your face—the blushing effect. How does that happen?

Later on, I'll cover the importance of the microbiome—the trillions of microbes that make your body their home in (mostly) symbiosis. They thrive largely in your gut, where they make chemicals that communicate with the brain through nerves and hormones. At the center of this two-way highway is the vagus ("wandering") nerve, which extends from your brain stem down to the abdomen. We often don't think about the strong link between our gut and brain (and skin, for that matter), but it's there and is just as active and energetic as other indelible connections. The so-called gut-brain-skin axis is one of the hottest areas of scientific study today. Indeed, what's going on in your gut shows up on your skin—and in your head.

So, picture all of your internal organs and glands as being connected to those meridians, of which there are twelve principal ones. They run on both sides of the body, each side mirroring the other, and each meridian corresponds to an organ or gland. The meridians originate from different parts of the brain and unfurl through different parts of the hands and feet. As you can likely guess, this provides the foundation for acupuncture, as most acupuncture (and acupressure) points lie on a meridian. One can stimulate these points using acupuncture needles (or acupressure) and help correct (adjust) and rebalance the flow of energy and blood flow.

Let me give you an example to bring this home for you. If your gallbladder or liver is not functioning properly, you might not know it until you develop a headache. You see, the meridian lines for your liver and gallbladder run through the neck up by the temples and through the optic nerve. When these organs are weak, those meridian lines can trigger tightness in the neck muscles that then manifests in a headache. And if you find yourself instinctively rubbing your temples, forehead, or back of the head at the base of your skull, you're performing a little acupressure on yourself as you rub over those meridians. You may find relief, but not for long if you don't treat the source of the actual pain—the liver and/or gallbladder.

When I work with patients in my practice, one of my first orders of business is to find where their weaknesses are. Which organs or glands are not acting up to code? Where's the source of the problem? Given my thirty-plus years of experience, it doesn't take long for me to pinpoint the root cause of their pain. Using a combination of a physical exam with hands-on muscle testing, questions about their diet and lifestyle, and basic labs (e.g., blood pressure, oral pH, zinc status), I can get a detailed picture pretty quickly. Of course, the exact location of their headache tells me a lot. It gives me an idea of where their primary problem likely resides. This is why I call headaches the canaries in the coal mine. They tell you where the origin of your pain is really coming from so you can zero in on that area and treat it for good.

Unlike the laundry list of potential causes for headaches, there are only seven pain patterns in all headaches that I've documented in my practice through my decades-long work with patients. And I have yet to treat someone whose headache doesn't fall into one of those pain patterns. Granted, I might not be a research scientist who has conducted double-blind, placebo-controlled studies on these pain patterns, but my discoveries follow the recorded science to date. Nothing is more convincing to me than the success of ending pain for thousands of patients.

Some of my patients like to call me a magician, but I don't see myself as that. I'm not employing any wizardry or the art of illusion. There's no doubt some art to my practice as I sleuth through the clues of a patient's symptoms and history to perform the right exam, arrive at a proper diagnosis, and treat it accordingly. But my work stems from applying long-established knowledge to patients on an individual level and their unique physiology, down to their blood type and even DNA. Don't panic: I won't be asking you to order a genome sequencing test. It can help to know your blood type, but you can confidently figure that out from dietary clues (see Chapter 12).

Now, let's get to the science of pain, which provides a great foundation for comprehending the seven pain patterns in detail.

CHAPTER 2

THE SCIENCE OF PAIN

The Surprising How of Hurt

When Gail sought medical help for her daily left-sided headaches, she was told they were likely due to an autoimmune condition called temporal arteritis. She had seen many doctors before me and was in the process of confirming her diagnosis. Temporal arteritis, also called giant cell arteritis, is a condition in which the body has begun to attack the arteries, in this case on the left side of the head. Lab tests including her markers of inflammation, which were high, substantiated the initial diagnosis. To confirm it, she was scheduled to undergo a painful biopsy of the artery on the left side of her head. Luckily, she got to me before that procedure, which could have led her to a lifetime reliance on potent immune-suppressing medications.

Although she did not disclose any stomach or digestive discomfort on her intake form for me, I was confident in knowing that almost any pain on the left side of the head would be caused by a stomach condition. I evaluated her with that in mind, noting that she had weakness and tenderness in the left upper chest area (left clavicular region of the pectoral muscle). She had tenderness in the left jaw muscles. Her mouth's pH was very acidic (at 6.2) because her digestion was not working properly. She had chronic tension between the shoulders (T5 area). And further tests revealed that she had low stomach acid (hydrochloric acid, or HCl), which contributed to poor digestion. No sooner did I start her on a natural supplement to address the hydrochloric acid deficiency than the headaches lifted. When she returned one month later, she was headache-free and the lab markers previously pointing to inflammation and an autoimmune condition had also cleared up and normalized.

Another patient, Marian, also came to me complaining of left-sided headaches that had plagued her for 25 years. I found it very interesting that in her case, the primary inhibitor to optimal stomach function was the perfume she had been wearing daily. She promptly quit wearing that perfume and has not had a headache in the past decade. Unfortunately, since contents are not required to be listed, it can be hard to determine which ingredient causes the headaches. Pay attention to symptoms of sneezing, brain fog, or cravings when your fragrance is applied.

To gain an understanding of the connection between the pain patterns in your head and various organs and glands, let's consider the science of pain to begin with.

THE PATHOLOGY OF PAIN

When I drum up a useful analogy to describe the human body in terms of its interconnectedness, I see a giant orb web—a large circular cobweb with threads radiating from a central point and crossed by radial links spiraling in from the edge. It's neat and tidy, a brilliant design by nature that's geometrically balanced and symmetrical. But if you pull ever so delicately on one corner of the orb, guess what happens: the whole thing will move because it's all tied together. You can't just disrupt one small thread and not affect the whole thing to a degree. And it's an apt way of thinking about the human body and its relationship with pain—a pull on the body in one place that shifts the entire enterprise. Granted, that's an oversimplification because with the human body, there are often redundancies, safeguards, and checks and balances that help prevent a glitch in one area from adversely impacting other areas, but you get my point.

Pain is a fascinating reality of living in the animal kingdom. And even the word "pain" has intriguing origins. It comes from the Latin word *poena*, which means "penalty" or "punishment." In Greek mythology, Poena (or Poine) is the spirit of punishment, recompense, or vengeance; this personified spirit is also the attendant to Nemesis, the goddess of divine retribution. You might assume pain implies revenge based on this etymology, but I don't interpret it that way. Pain serves a mighty purpose: to tell us what we must tend to, what to avoid (e.g., hot stove, allergenic food), and when to rest up. Pain is not only one of our greatest teachers but the compass to self-preservation. It's perhaps the most influential force for behavioral change. If you can stop pain through a simple change in how you go about your day-to-day life, my guess is you'll make the necessary shifts.

Although most of us grew up thinking that pain could always be tied to a physical ailment or structural problem within the body, we know much differently now thanks to newer technologies that allow us to better quantify and qualify pain even when we can't "see" it. Look no further than the experience of real pain that people can go through after emotional stress or trauma. There's no structural or physical damage to ascribe to the pain, but the pain is real. For a more extreme example, consider those who've lost a limb yet continue to sense pain from that body part no longer there—a bewildering occurrence called *phantom limb syndrome*. This happens when the nerve endings at the site of the lost arm or leg keep sending the brain pain signals, making the brain erroneously think the limb is still there. The brain is, as it were, essentially duped and the mix-up in nervous system signals leaves the person in agony.

Pain and emotions are uniquely tied together, and not just metaphorically.[1] They are also tied in the brain's circuitry, overlapping and influencing one another. Just as pain can affect your emotions, your emotions can affect your pain. When you're grumpy or down, you're likely going to feel more pain—your experience of pain is magnified. New research has gone so far as to show that the circuitry in the brain responsible for pleasure and motivation is changed by the experience of pain, particularly when it's chronic and relentless, as is the case for many headache sufferers.[2]

Basically, what research is demonstrating is that chronic pain makes one more sensitive to pain, which is a proverbial vicious cycle. Those who develop headaches on a regular basis are much more likely to report higher levels of pain from other conditions or injuries. Their "set point" for pain—the range in which they can tolerate pain—is low compared to someone who can tolerate higher levels of pain without disrupting their life too much. We each have a baseline tolerance for pain before we seek solutions. We each have ways to cope within that range, hoping that it doesn't exceed our limit and establish a new set point. Set points vary tremendously among people, from genetics and physiology to individual experiences of pain in the past, and even our *perceptions* of pain stemming from a confluence of emotions and mental states. Take two people and expose them to the same exact pain-inducing situation and they will have different experiences. One might describe the level of pain on a scale of 1 to 10 (10 being high) as an 8, whereas the other individual will give it a 5. Such a discrepancy may seem questionable or doubtful, but that's the nature of pain.

Set points in general are talked about in the context of many biological systems. Set point theory first grew out of conversations about weight—there are biological control methods that actively regulate weight toward a predetermined number for each person. The body prefers to stay within a certain range of weight, and it will do whatever it can to remain in that "home" range, barring any extreme over- or undereating for a prolonged period. A good question: Can you change your set point for pain? The short answer is yes. Just as you can change your set point for weight (up or down) with the right diet and exercise regimen to make over your metabolism, you can raise or lower your tolerance for pain with the right protocol attuned to your body and its needs, and that's exactly what we're going to do. Part of this retooling of your pain set point is leveraging your brain's "plastic" powers. Let me explain.

Scientists who study pain have been at the forefront of a burgeoning area in medicine that seeks to understand how the brain can change its wiring. It's called *neuroplasticity*, defined as the ability of neural networks in the brain to change in response to injury, learning, or experience.[3] The brain can "rewire" itself to function in some way different from how it did before. This helps explain how we can grow new networks throughout our lives, including the birth of new brain cells that can wire and fire together in the creation of novel networks. When stroke victims can recover some of their mental faculties and physical feats, that's neuroplasticity at work. Put simply, the brain is not fixed, and you're not doomed to run out of the brain cells you were born with, assuming you take care of your brain to promote healthy neuroplasticity.

As mentioned, the brain has no pain center—it lacks nerves to detect damage or the threat of damage to the body. Such nerves are called nociceptors (*noci* is Latin for "harm"), and they are responsible for sending pain signals to the spinal cord and brain. These specialized nerve endings are located close to the spine, and their fibers extend into other parts of the body and organs, including the skin. They respond to basic kinds of painful, threatening triggers, such as extreme heat or cold, pressure, certain chemicals, and damage. Nociceptors then convey the hurt to the brain via the spinal cord. In response, higher-order neurons in the brain's cortex translate the incoming message as pain.

The ultimate conundrum: How can pain signals that become physical sensations of pain get their start in emotions? The answer lies in the overlap of sensory perception in the brain and its processing of those emotions. In other words, the part of the brain associated with sensory perception is the same space that takes center stage in handling your emotional state. Pure nociception from physical damage is straightforward, but the form of pain attached to unpleasant emotions is a different beast. If that sounds implausible, consider this: Studies show that multiple regions are activated in response to painful stimuli—not just one.[4] Thanks to neuroimaging studies, we know that the brain processes physical pain and emotional distress in the same regions.[5] And the regions triggered are also involved with emotion, memory, cognition, and decision-making. Such complex cross-linkage is how scientists explain why individuals who suffer from depression often experience more pain in daily life. Studies have tested this out by inducing a low mood in otherwise normal (non-depressed) research subjects, who then reported a lower tolerance for pain (and higher levels of pain).[6]

MERIDIANS MAY HOLD THE ANSWER

Nuances to how pain behaves and is cultivated have everything to do with those meridians. Studies in recent years have finally revealed the stunning value in acupuncture to bolster the "invisible" connections throughout the body that invigorate its "web-like" structure and tether virtually every cell, tissue, organ, and gland to the nervous system. In 2018, a consortium of scientists from around the world published a large meta-analysis study that showed acupuncture is indeed effective for the treatment of chronic pain, especially musculoskeletal, headache, and osteoarthritis pain.[7] The study was led by none other than our renowned Memorial Sloan Kettering Cancer Center in New York, and it concluded that "[t]reatment effects of acupuncture persist over time and cannot be explained solely in terms of placebo effects." The researchers were careful in making sure to include experiments with sham acupuncture and no acupuncture. Sham acupuncture is what it sounds like: researchers "pretend" to perform acupuncture on subjects, but they don't actually hit the right spots on the meridians or they don't penetrate deep enough to elicit a response. The practitioner goes through the motions without giving the treatment, and the patient is oblivious to whether or not they are receiving the simulated fake or the authentic procedure. Sham acupuncture acts as a control to compare against subjects who receive the real deal. Sadly, for the sham recipients, no benefit was enjoyed.

Other studies have also demonstrated the pain-reducing effects of acupuncture and tried to figure out the mechanisms behind its power.[8] Amazingly, these studies increasingly illustrate that manipulating the meridians changes the brain in remarkable ways—from what it senses from the body to how it regulates its own internal neurochemistry that in turn affects pain signaling. In other words, acupuncture induces changes in the nervous system and brain—effects that include changing the levels of chemical messengers ("neurotransmitters"), which are partly responsible for the feeling of pain. The treatment also adjusts cell activity in the muscles and skin, thereby affecting certain signaling molecules that travel to the brain.

Scientists can now measure these changes in the brain and, in some cases, even visualize them using high-tech imaging techniques (e.g., MRI and PET scans). In one particularly provocative study led by a team of researchers at the University of Michigan and funded by the U.S. Department of the Army and the National Institutes of Health, they looked at the reaction of acupuncture on opioid receptors in the brains of patients who have chronic pain from fibromyalgia.[9] As you can imagine, opioid receptors are directly linked to sensations of pain and, conversely, pain relief and analgesic effects. In particular, the researchers showed that the treatment increases the binding availability of certain opioid receptors in regions of the brain that process and dampen pain signals. These regions include the cingulate cortex, the insula, the caudate, the thalamus, and the ancient amygdala. One of the prevailing theories as to what's going on is that acupuncture not only changes the brain and its cellular connections but boosts the supply of circulating natural analgesics, which then talk to the brain, positively affecting its short- and long-term ability to regulate pain.

I'm not teaching you how to perform acupuncture on yourself in this book. But we are going to use this very effective insight to help you find solutions. The lesson here is the following: All of your organs and tissues are bridged to your brain through the intricacies of your nervous system, which includes your spinal cord and brain. And how those organs and tissues are functioning will impact the reactions in the nervous system and response from the brain. If something is off-kilter somewhere, that imbalance can easily manifest as a headache. Improved stomach function, for instance, will improve the meridian that flows from the stomach to the brain. Similarly, when you address the gallbladder meridian, which happens to be one of the longest and most complex meridians that controls body movement, the brain, the gut, the autonomic nervous system, and cognition, you can support optimal functioning of all those important parts of the body. This dominating meridian travels from the eyes, brain, and neck down to the fourth toe. As an aside, and which we'll explore in detail later, the gallbladder meridian is also the main meridian system that regulates the vagus nerve, so it has a lot to do with the connection between your gut, your brain, and even your entire immune system, or what's called the "seventh sense."

IS THE FOOD YOU EAT GOING TO YOUR HEAD?

Some of the other connections we'll be exploring in this book and that tie into risk for headaches may seem elusive until you connect the dots. I realize that it can be hard to follow the connection between what you eat and brain function, but the science is already well established. What you eat directly and indirectly affects the structure and function of your brain. Case in point: Sugar consumption, especially that from refined sugars, will interfere with insulin signaling, promote inflammation, and fuel the kind of stress on the body and brain that opens the door for pain to pay a visit in the form of a headache. Many ingredients can be problematic too, inciting a cascade of effects that ultimately land in your throbbing head.

An abundance of nutrients and non-nutrients, from good ones (like fiber) to bad ones (like pesticides), can affect your brain, its neuronal function and processes through synaptic plasticity, and your emotions. There's even a molecular basis for the effects of food on the brain and the brain's response to "peripheral signals" coming in from food.[10] For decades, the medical field ignored—or shunned—any talk about the food-brain connection or, more precisely, the food-mood connection. Today, however, the burgeoning field of nutritional psychiatry is finding many correlations between poor nutrition and poor mental faculties, with measurable changes to the brain. And one of the brokers or dealers, so to speak, of those correlations is the gut.

According to Harvard Health, "the inner workings of your digestive system don't just help you digest food but also guide your emotions."[11] Eva Selhub, MD, writing for Harvard's Health Blog, goes on to state that the function of neurons in the gastrointestinal tract are under the influence of good bacteria that thrive in the gut and comprise your microbiome. These microbes *produce* neurotransmitters like serotonin, which helps regulate sleep and appetite. Serotonin is also involved with mediating your mood and inhibiting pain. We tend to think of serotonin as solely a "brain chemical," but a whopping 95 percent of this key neurotransmitter is made in your gastrointestinal tract. It must be balanced: low levels of serotonin are associated with depression; high levels can provoke anxiety, irritability, and restlessness.

Again, the key is to strike the right balance. Too much, or not enough, of anything will wreak havoc. As we'll see later on, serotonin imbalances can be one of the reasons for frontal headaches. I treat scores of patients with frontal headaches, and they are always surprised by the root cause of them because it's not where they'd automatically think: the stomach (not the eyes, as many presume). They may not have any stomach issues to complain about—their pain's origin is silent. But no sooner do we work together to heal their stomach function than their headaches vanish. What a tangled web the body weaves!

I've given you a lot to think about in this chapter, and we're just getting started. Before we do a deep dive into unlocking your head's unique pain through an understanding of all seven pain patterns, let's first cover the smoking guns to any kind of headache. No matter what type of headache haunts you, knowing the top dietary, environmental, and emotional triggers will go a long way to help you begin to heal.

CHAPTER 3

SMOKING GUNS TO ANY KIND OF HEADACHE

Dietary, Environmental, and Emotional Triggers

The number of triggers to a headache that you encounter from the moment you get out of bed is countless. Staggering! Think about all the exposures that begin the day. The following list is not meant to frighten you, but it puts daily life into a perspective most people don't consider when it comes to understanding the inputs to their pain.

First, there's the bathroom, where common chemical ingredients in toiletries and cosmetics can elicit a biological response and provoke weaknesses in organs and systems. Take a look at the list of ingredients in your favorite products, from shampoos and body washes to makeup and beauty products. Can you understand them all or even pronounce them?

Second, there's the kitchen, where you're faced with problematic food ingredients and questionable drinking water, not to mention everyday household goods, furniture, children's toys, and cleaning products that could be emitting noxious, invisible chemicals. More than 86,000 industrial chemicals and counting are allowed for use in the U.S.—and for the vast majority of these chemicals, *their toxicity to human health is unknown*; only five harmful chemicals have been banned in the U.S. since 1976, yet many of these persist in the environment today.[1] New legislation passed in 2016, which was hailed as the first overhaul to the Toxic Substances Control Act of 1976, requires the Environmental Protection Agency to test tens of thousands of unregulated chemicals currently on the market, plus the new chemicals (about 2,000) that come out each year.[2] But here's the catch: At a pace of reviewing at least 20 chemicals at a time, it will take the EPA centuries to finish the job. Meanwhile, these chemicals are allowed to be used.

Lastly, there's your commute to work through polluted air and a full day of stressors. All along, you're managing the general stress of life and worries about work, family, money, general health, the future, and so on. Just reading this might be stressing you out!

Throughout Part II (coming up), we'll be going into fine detail about the seven pain patterns and learn about triggers that exacerbate headaches. Before we get to that section, however, I want to prime you with some information about three categories of culprits that everyone should be aware of. I can't cover every potential offender, but there's plenty to be said about some of the most ubiquitous ones in modern life. Let's start with where you can likely make the biggest impact in your habits to relieve your headaches: *diet.*

DIETARY DEVILS

Raise your hand if you fell prey to the low-fat/non-fat craze of the 1990s (I just raised mine). The "fat-phobic" fad was based on the false belief that dietary fat fattened people up, so food manufacturers started to replace dietary fat with other ingredients, notably refined carbohydrates and sugar or highly processed sugar in the form of high-fructose corn syrup.

Remember the brand SnackWell's? They made America's best-selling cookie in 1995, but the brand was discontinued in 2022. They were the scene-stealing boxes back in their heyday. Did we really think we could get away with guiltless cookies, cakes, and "Devil's Food Cookie Cakes"? SnackWell's was just one of many brands making and promoting fat-free packaged goods to capitalize on the trend to avoid dietary fat. But eliminating the fat meant substituting with refined carbohydrates. It's no mystery now that our obesity epidemic really took off the more sugar—not fat—we consumed, and the number of people with diabetes has tripled in the past three decades.

Don't feel bad if you too fell prey to the trend and misinformation. *We all did.* I was bodybuilding at the time and my diet was regularly evaluated at over 5,000 calories, with 75 percent coming from carbohydrates, 20 percent from protein, and a mere 5 percent from fats. My college classmates virtually bowed to these "amazing numbers." Yet I had massive blood sugar swings and an average of 14 percent body fat, which is high for a bodybuilding young man. Years later, as my understanding of the body improved and I began to race mountain bikes—an aerobic, fat-metabolizing sport—I increased my intake of good fats to about 30 percent of my calories. As you can imagine, it became easier to eat "normal" foods and to avoid the fat-free fare. My blood sugar stabilized. My sleep deepened. And my body fat lowered to 6 percent and stayed there.

Here's the memo that didn't go around in the '90s: Consumption of quality fats *stabilizes* blood sugar. They are the precursors for hormones and reduce inflammation. And let's not forget that they *taste* good too. In the program, I'll show you how to bring high-quality fats into your diet. You can start simply by welcoming raw nuts and seeds, reaching for healthy oils like olive and avocado oil, and seeking clean, cold-water fish to further reduce inflammation, stabilize energy, and enjoy happy hormones.

When energy (blood sugar) is stable, cravings go down. Therefore, discipline goes up and weight plummets—benefits most people could use. It's a win-win!

Sugar is my #1 public enemy in the dietary department. Over the past century, but particularly in the past fifty years, sugar consumption in the U.S. has gone up steadily. Such a surge has corresponded with higher rates of obesity and diabetes. Here's another way of taking in the scope of the problem: In 1940, roughly one in every 400 people in the U.S. was diabetic. Today, one in every nine is diabetic, with one in three of people over 65 suffering some sort of metabolic dysfunction.[3] Sugar consumption accelerated around 1980, when the obesity epidemic took off, and the diabetes epidemic began about a decade later, in the 1990s. Although it may seem intuitive to think the main source of more sugar has come from classic treats, pastries, packaged and processed goods, and traditional desserts, it's the *liquid* calories that have been so impactful. Sugary drinks account for nearly half (46 percent) of the added sugars in the American diet and are the largest source of added sugars for all age groups.[4] Snacks and sweets are the second largest source, contributing 31 percent of added sugars.

It amazes me how long it can take for the truth to come out. It takes an average of about seventeen years for revealing data collected in research studies, *including* data that exposes inefficacy and/or a signal of harm, to enter your doctor's daily routine.[5] That's a long time lag between bench to bedside. But sometimes that lag can actually be worse, and further complicated by nefarious characters in industries with hidden agendas. In 2016, for instance, a new article for *JAMA Internal Medicine* laid bare a shocking discovery: The sugar industry quietly funded research in the 1960s that "downplayed the risks of sugar and highlighted the hazards of fat" when it came to heart health.[6] A powerful sugar lobby group called the Sugar Research Foundation (now called the Sugar Association) sponsored research by Harvard scientists to "refute" concerns about sugar's possible role in heart disease. And the Ivy League researchers published their findings in 1967 in one of our most prestigious peer-reviewed journals, the *New England Journal of Medicine*.[7] Without disclosing their funding by the sugar industry, they pointed the finger at fat and cholesterol as the problem fueling coronary heart disease.

The paper was a review critical of certain studies done to implicate sugar. But it was clearly biased and framed by the interests of the sugar lobby. And it took another fifty years for us to come to our senses and realize the sugar industry has been secretly influencing how we should eat. When you get a paper published in such a prominent journal, the message can be hard to deny or debate. When Harvard scientists and the *New England Journal of Medicine* tell you to cut the fat, you listen, and so does *your doctor!*

SUGAR MAY BE A GREAT WAY TO GET A HEADACHE

Many books have been written about the ravages of sugar on the body and brain. In brief, too much sugar will create imbalances in blood sugar, fan the flames of systemic inflammation, bomb your microbiome, and generally wreak havoc on your healthy physiology. All of these effects have direct ties to your risk of a headache. There are two big effects of sugar that I want to point out and that will shape the conversation going forward: sugar gives and takes away.

For starters, sugar is a nutrient thief. Sugar leaches zinc and B vitamins, especially B1 (thiamine). The resulting deficiencies have multiple sweeping effects. As an anti-inflammatory and antioxidant trace element, zinc is a cofactor for antioxidant enzymes that play a key role in neuronal signaling. It's crucial for the growth, development, and maintenance of immune function.

WHITE CLOUDS IN THE FINGERNAILS MAY BE A SIGN OF HEADACHE RISK

Zinc has wide-ranging effects other than just immunity, reaching all organs and cell types. Zinc is necessary for many hormonal, stress tolerance, and mental and emotional functions. So, a deficiency can not only cause under-functioning of the immune system but also an underperformance of hormones, brain chemistry, and stress tolerance. The stomach also needs zinc to make the acid that breaks down food.

The zinc deficiency problem gets exaggerated by stress, and the fact our soils are predominantly mineral-deficient means it can be hard to make up the difference through a standard diet unless you seek out zinc-rich foods. Viral infections can also use up zinc stores in your body. You can sometimes see nutrient deficiencies like that of zinc in fingernails. Often, little white clouds will show up. You can watch the white clouds grow out, and unless the zinc deficiency is remedied, more white clouds will emerge (with your headaches).

As we'll see later on, excellent sources of zinc include seafood (especially oysters), pumpkin seeds, poultry, red meat, nuts, legumes, and fortified cereals (so long as those cereals are produced from organic whole grains—see below about glyphosate). In 2023, a study of more than 11,000 Americans published in the journal *Headache* showed that dietary zinc intake is inversely related to migraine risk: those with both high dietary zinc and zinc supplementation showed the lowest number of headaches.[8] We need to be intentional about zinc foods, as well as take a good zinc supplement, as the soils our vegetables are grown in tend to be zinc- and mineral-deficient.

Zinc deficiency can cause left-sided, frontal, bitemporal, and possibly tension headaches. If you experience more than one of these, chances are pretty good that you would do well to add a good zinc supplement to your daily regimen. I routinely come across zinc deficiencies in my patients—upwards of 199 for every 200 initial patient encounters. According to an Australian group, "Zinc deficiency is strikingly common, affecting up to a quarter of the population in developing countries."[9]

Signs of a zinc deficiency:

1. *White clouds / spots in the fingernails*
2. *Sickness that comes on premenstrually*
3. *Frontal or left-sided headaches*
4. *Headaches on both sides of the head (bitemporal)*
5. *Loss of smell and / or taste*
6. *Poor tolerance of stress*
7. *Sugar cravings*
8. *Exposure to toxins, chemicals, or even tattoo ink that can exaggerate zinc deficiency*
9. *Chemical sensitivities (i.e., sneezing around perfumes or toxins)*
10. *Low levels of testosterone or other hormones*
11. *Gas, bloating, discomfort, or brain fog after meals (potential leaky gut barrier symptoms—see below)*
12. *Achilles tendonitis (Achilles irritation and even ruptures are typically caused by viral weakness.)*
13. *If your child is a finicky eater, they are likely low in zinc. (We stock a liquid form of zinc for this reason. It will often expand the child's palate toward healthier vegetables and less sugar.)*

COULD B VITAMINS STABILIZE YOUR MOOD AND REDUCE HEADACHES?

A B1 deficiency can be detrimental to stomach function, thyroid function, hormones, and liver function. When any of these areas are not performing up to speed, headaches are a common outcome. I often document patients whose B1 deficiency is caused not only by too much sugar consumption (and birth control pills) but overuse of alcohol. Alcohol-induced thiamine deficiency is well established in the medical literature. Vitamin B6 (pyridoxal-5-phosphate) is also compromised by alcohol; B6 is prominently needed for most brain chemical pathways. Therefore, a deficiency can lead to mental uncertainty and instability, as the neurotransmitters are often wildly out of balance.

Signs of a B1 (thiamine) deficiency:

1. *Headache on both sides (temples)*
2. *Headache in the front or on the left side*
3. *Headache in the back of the head*
4. *Sluggish metabolism*
5. *Mitral valve prolapse conditions (underperforming heart)*
6. *Low back pain in the center of the beltline*
7. *Low thyroid function*
8. *Pain/weakness in the gluteus medius muscle (which stabilizes our pelvis when we walk, run, or stand)*

ARE YOU FEEDING BAD BUGS?

Now, how does sugar "give," as I mentioned above? It clearly takes away from critical nutrients and minerals, but sugar will typically *feed* yeast overgrowth in the body. Unfortunately, when yeast flourishes, it then perpetuates sugar cravings. Many itch conditions are symptoms of yeast overgrowth. Signs of overgrowth can also be pain in the front of the shoulder, pain near the tailbone (sacrum or sacroiliac joint), soft bowel movements, pain near the outer knee, brain fog, and increased gut permeability. This means that toxins may penetrate through the intestinal lining into the bloodstream, then trigger inflammation and inflammatory conditions like arthritis.

Let me pause here to say a few things about "leaky gut," or what I prefer to call *intestinal permeability*. A single layer of epithelial cells lines your gastrointestinal tract. The intestinal lining is the body's largest mucosal surface, and it has three main functions:

1. It serves as the vehicle by which you obtain nutrients from the foods you eat.
2. It blocks the entrance into the bloodstream of potentially harmful particles, chemicals, and organisms that can pose a threat to your health.
3. It's the home to specialized cells that patrol and present to the immune system suspected invaders. The immune system provides chemicals called immunoglobulins that bind to foreign proteins to protect the body from them.

The body uses two pathways to absorb nutrients from the gut. One moves nutrients *through* the epithelial cells (transcellular); the other moves nutrients *between* the epithelial cells (paracellular). The connections between cells are called tight junctions, and as you can imagine, each of these complex, exceedingly small intersections is regulated. If they somehow become compromised and overly permeable, a condition called "leaky gut" develops. And because these junctions act as gatekeepers—keeping potential threats that will provoke the immune system out—they greatly influence levels of inflammation.

We in the medical community now know that when your intestinal barrier is damaged, a spectrum of health challenges can result, not the least of which is chronic headaches. Minerals can tighten the junctions; stress can open the junctions. What happens is that when these tight junctions are compromised, undigested food particles, cellular debris, and bacterial components can sneak by to stir trouble in the bloodstream, with downstream effects that manifest in headaches. This is largely why diet can be such an interventional powerhouse in healing from headaches. Heal your diet, heal your gut, heal your head!

SPICES COULD DAMAGE THE BRAIN

I should mention one insulting ingredient in particular that has gained notoriety and that we'd all do well to avoid: monosodium glutamate (MSG), a popular flavor enhancer. The headache pattern caused by MSG can be varied and is usually an exaggeration of another problem elsewhere. So, unfortunately, if your headaches are brought on by sauces or spices, you may also need to study one of the following chapters in Part II that best describes the location of your headaches.

Years ago, there was a commercial promoting MSG in a product aptly called Ac'cent (it's still sold today). It showed an otherwise lovely field of flowers as a dull black-and-white picture. Then Ac'cent was sprinkled on the flowers. Voila! The dull flowers suddenly came to life, becoming brilliantly colorful and vibrant. That is what MSG does to food and why it is commonly used by even some very high-end restaurants. Unfortunately, the neurotoxic component glutamate is also formed in the creation of many sauces and spices. This nerve killer can lead to headaches, as well as depression and memory loss. I realize that the scientific literature is a mixed bag on MSG. According to health authorities, MSG is "generally recognized as safe" (GRAS). But why have any dose of a neurotoxin? Granted, MSG is naturally present in many foods, from animal-based proteins (including meat, fish, eggs, and seafood) to aged cheeses, vegetables, nuts, and some fruits. But I'm less concerned about those natural sources of MSG than the kind found in highly processed meats, sauces, condiments, dressings, and premade and packaged foods.

Sneaky sources of MSG:

1. *Fast food*
2. *Seasonings, seasoning blends (e.g., taco seasoning packets), fish and meat rubs, bouillon cubes*
3. *Processed meats (e.g., sausages, smoked meats, pepperoni, beef jerky, hot dogs, lunch and deli meats, cured ham, beef/meat sticks)*
4. *Chips and snack foods*
5. *"Low-sodium" products*
6. *Frozen meals, including frozen pizzas, frozen breakfast meals, and frozen mac and cheese*
7. *Soup products, including canned soups (famous chicken noodle!), soup mixes, and dried soup mixes*
8. *Commercial sauces (including soy sauce, fish sauce, and tomato-based sauces), condiments (e.g., ketchup, mayonnaise, BBQ sauce, mustard), dressings, and gravies*
9. *Grape- and tomato-based juices*
10. *Instant noodles products*

> *Note: In addition to "monosodium glutamate" on the label, be on the lookout for other flavor enhancers that may be code for MSG:*
>
> 1. *Autolyzed yeast*
> 2. *Hydrolyzed vegetable protein*
> 3. *Hydrolyzed yeast*
> 4. *Protein isolate*
> 5. *Soy extracts*
> 6. *Yeast extract*

Historically, people sensitive to MSG have been labeled as victims of "Chinese Restaurant Syndrome," as MSG is often found in soy sauce and Asian fare. When Robert Ho Man Kwok, a Cantonese-born doctor who immigrated to the U.S., wrote a letter headlined "Chinese-Restaurant Syndrome" in 1968 to the *New England Journal of Medicine* in which he explained that he regularly got sick after consuming Chinese food, the unfortunate moniker stuck despite a change in nomenclature to "MSG symptom complex," or MSC.[10] Ever since that publication, the link between MSG and certain ailments, headaches being among the top of the list, has been debated ad nauseam. In addition to headaches, the chemical has been linked to metabolic disorders, obesity, and brain toxicity.

If you get headaches after consuming Asian food, barbeque sauce, or any other food with spices or sauce, you are likely reacting to an MSG (glutamate) derivative. You would do well to avoid these. People who have sustained one or more concussions tend to be more sensitive to MSG, as the brain is presumably producing glutamate because of the injury. When nerves die, as happens in a concussion, glutamate is liberated from damaged neurons, contributing to many of the symptoms people suffer from after a head injury. This is why fish oil products high in DHA omega-3 fatty acids can be helpful both to prevent and recover from head injuries.

Surprise: Low-sodium soy sauce is not the answer. It has more MSG because it's used to replace the sodium. I have yet to find a healthy substitute, as many similarly fermented products still behave as MSG in the brain. For sushi, as a substitute, I mix wasabi into lemon juice with ginger for my dip. Both wasabi and ginger are very anti-parasitic, which potentially kills parasites in the raw fish.

ENVIRONMENTAL EVIL

It would be beyond the scope of this book to outline every potential environmental insult you encounter that could be driving your headaches. We live in a sea of chemicals today in the air we breathe, the water we drink, the food we eat, and the things we put on our bodies, like lotions and perfumes. Sometimes, it's easy to spot a culprit disrupting our normal biology. If a fragrance or cologne we wear always triggers a headache, that's an easy fix. But often, the culprits are hidden and challenging to spot. There's one villain in particular that has found its way throughout the food chain that deserves our attention. I mentioned it earlier: glyphosate. This is the main active ingredient in many weed killers (herbicides), including Bayer's popular Roundup. More than 80 percent of Americans have been recently exposed.

Glyphosate was first registered for use in 1974 and has since become the most widely used herbicide to control plant growth in farming and gardening. In the U.S., it is used as a pre-harvest treatment. And while it's primarily used for grains like wheat, corn, oats, and soy, it lands in more than 750 products.[11]

Concerns are on the rise about glyphosate's link to rising cancer rates, especially lymphomas. It's also been associated with reproductive problems, birth defects, kidney disease, and liver damage, where it inhibits bile production, thereby causing gallbladder congestion and right-sided headaches.

We're exposed to this chemical through a variety of channels: when we use it on lawns and plants, when it's in the air, and when we consume it in foods and even drinking water. The chemical is so ubiquitous that it's been found in organic foods, non-GMO foods, and 75 percent of air and rain samples (it lands in non-GMO foods like wheat and oats because it is used as a pre-harvest desiccant, so it's left in the soil). Common food products that have tested positive for glyphosate include granola, cereals, chips, cookies, whole and instant oats, orange juice, ice cream, and snack bars. Chances are, your urine would test positive for it (a 2017 study led by UC San Diego discovered that it's regularly found in human urine).[12]

Glyphosate does more than kill weeds and puts us in danger through our exposure to it. Glyphosate can profoundly impact a crop's ability to absorb nutrients from the soil, so those crops are rendered less nutrient-dense. What's more, glyphosate has antibiotic properties that kill good bacteria in the soil and in our guts. When it disrupts beneficial bacteria in our microbiome, it interferes with the production of essential amino acids such as tryptophan, a serotonin precursor, and promotes the production of p-cresol, a compound that interferes with the metabolism of other "xenobiotics" or environmental chemicals. As a result, the person becomes more vulnerable to their toxic effects. Even vitamin D3 activation in the liver may be adversely impacted by glyphosate's effect on liver enzymes. Some have even argued that vitamin D deficiencies could partly be explained by exposure to glyphosate.

Many countries have banned or restricted the use of glyphosate due to the growing concerns about its toxicity. But one thing is for sure: We should all avoid it (I'll be sharing tips for doing just that later on). Its extensive effects on the body have everything to do with the risk of a headache. As you'll soon learn in the next chapter, by far, the most consistent trigger I see for right-sided headaches is—you guessed it—glyphosate, due to its compromising impact on gallbladder function.

EMOTIONAL VILLAINS

Ana was having lunch in Peru when her lunchmate shared some heavy gossip about Ana herself. It caused an immediate violent stress reaction that manifested as pain in the top and front of her head. Three weeks later, when she finally came to get treated in my office, the pain had barely diminished. She had tried a migraine medication that she threw up within 15 minutes and another IV medication that offered no help, unfortunately. Given her story, I knew we were dealing with an overzealous stress response. I used a technique to treat the emotions (a version of which you can see at www.HeadacheAdvantage.com), and her head pain was gone immediately. On this website, you'll find links to prior headache-oriented podcasts, as well as potential supplement protocols for each of the seven headache patterns.

Emotions can get in the way of a lot—how we choose to eat, how well we sleep, how much we move and exercise, how we relate with others, how we cope with stress, how our bodies *respond* to that stress…and so on. Our emotions are like the metaphorical connective tissues in our lives, linking and coordinating our behavior and physiological states. Countless studies have tracked different emotions to the activation of many bodily systems—the cardiovascular, neuroendocrine, musculoskeletal, and autonomic nervous systems, the latter of which consists of the sympathetic and parasympathetic.[13]

The sympathetic nervous system is your body's fight-or-flight programming—the one that accelerates your pulse and ups blood pressure to divert blood away from digestion and toward your brain and muscles. It keeps you alert and mentally adept. The parasympathetic nervous system, on the other hand, is your rest-and-digest programming that allows you to rebuild, repair, and sleep. Depending on what you're doing and how you're feeling, either your sympathetic or parasympathetic system is dominating.

Emotions are not only tied to bodily states, which is what gives rise to things like a racing heart when excited or trembling hands and tight muscles when nervous, but our emotions correlate with organs too. Low self-esteem and disgust, for instance, correlate with the stomach; anger and frustration correlate with the gallbladder. I realize that managing and addressing emotional issues and triggers can seem like an entirely different psychological endeavor, but I'm going to be giving you some shrink-free strategies to consider coming up in the program. Indeed, emotions are a silent trigger to many types of headaches. Once you gain control of them, release the trigger, and heal the weakness, you can end the headache.

I appreciate your motivation. You have now learned and implemented some key lifestyle changes. You now understand that:

**Pain is intended to elicit *change*.
You are not a victim.
You are designed to THRIVE.**

The advantage of pain in the head is that it can direct you to where your body needs help.

The advantage of reviews is that they direct people to trust a product.

Please take 60 seconds to click on a link below to leave an honest review of *The Headache Advantage* so that others will have the confidence to embrace this material.

Amazon/TheHeadacheAdvantage
Good Reads/TheHeadacheAdvantage

**Thank you for taking the time
share your valuable thoughts**

https://www.amazon.com/dp/B0DCNYNHKZ

PART II

UNLOCKING YOUR HEAD'S UNIQUE PAIN

CHAPTER 4

LEFT-SIDED HEADACHES

Problem in the Stomach

These are common characteristics among people who suffer from left-sided headaches, and the root cause is typically a problem in the stomach. Low stomach acid in particular is one of the prime causes I see routinely in my practice, even when the patient has no clue. But other issues in the stomach could also be at play, such as an ingredient you ingested that didn't agree with your stomach, a nutrient deficiency that impacts the stomach, or too much cortisol in your system, which will inhibit stomach function by lowering stomach acid. Go ahead: check all the boxes that apply to you.

Common Symptoms, Signs, and / or Characteristics Associated with Left-Sided Headaches

☐ *Left-sided head pain*
☐ *Pain between the shoulders (T5)*
☐ *Left jaw pain*
☐ *Pain at the top of the right or left ankle*
☐ *Inner elbow pain*
☐ *Wrist weakness*

- *Achy joints, especially the fingers*
- *Slow protein digestion / lack of regular bowel movements*
- *Allergies*
- *Weak immune system / chronic infections*
- *Being overly sympathetic*
- *Low self-esteem*
- *Symptoms worse between 7 and 9 AM*
- *Easily disgusted*
- *Despair*
- *Bad breath*
- *Burping*
- *Constipation*
- *Left-sided sinus congestion*
- *Upset stomach in the morning*
- *Sneezing after eating*
- *Feeling need to take acid-blocking medications and / or antacids*

The challenge can be in determining what is offending the stomach or what the stomach needs. This is why it helps to keep a log of your eating choices, so when a headache hits, you can identify a potential trigger. Did you eat wheat, dairy, or sugar? Did you experience an unusual stressor that spiked cortisol levels? Cortisol is your body's chief stress hormone that is uniquely tied to a lot of bodily functions and factors into appetite and hunger cues, metabolism, fat retention, inflammation, blood pressure, immunity, and recovery from an acutely stressful event. When you go through the program outlined in Part III, I'll be asking you to keep a journal so you can nail your triggers and become more attuned to your body and its needs.

> *If you frequently get headaches on the left side of the head, it's most likely rooted in the stomach, and low stomach acid could be the culprit.*

THE STOMACH'S ALARM MAY BE IN YOUR HEAD

Studying the pattern of the stomach acupuncture meridian (energy flow) is one of the things that led me to consider the stomach as the primary cause of left or frontal headaches. This meridian starts under the eye and goes through the chest area and down to the top of the ankle. Note that the stomach is located on the left side of the body, which is why some of the symptoms are predominantly on the left side. As I began to evaluate people with left-sided head pains, it panned out that every single one of them had some sort of stomach dysfunction. The late, great Dr. George Goodheart originally identified the correlation between poor stomach function and the clavicular portion of the pectoralis muscle. There will be tenderness in the belly of that muscle on the left when the stomach is not functioning optimally. The tenderness will dissolve when appropriate changes are made for the stomach.

You'll recall that Dr. Goodheart is the one who originally correlated many of the muscle-organ associations by identifying which acupuncture meridians went through the muscle. Interestingly, the meridians often go in the exact direction of the muscle fibers. One of my early mentors, Dr. Robert Blaich, conducted research in the 1980s to confirm Dr. Goodheart's muscle-organ correlations.[1] One of the ways he did this was by demonstrating the pectoral muscle weakness that occurred after irritating the stomach with ice-cold water. Ice water is said to temporarily inhibit proper stomach function. It was confirmed that the clavicular portion of the pectoral muscle consistently became conditionally inhibited when the stomach was challenged with ice water. This corroborated both the clavicular portion of the pectoral muscles with the stomach and Dr. Goodheart's fine work connecting muscle function, or lack thereof, with organ functioning. This correlation is now used clinically by thousands of doctors on a daily basis.

With all this in mind, areas where the stomach may refer pain could include the left side or front of the head, the jaw, the chest area (especially the left side), between the shoulders, and possibly the wrists or ankles.

> *When the stomach is not functioning properly, much of the body is not going to feel good.*

We all know that when our stomachs are under-functioning, much of the body is not happy. Digestion starts in the mouth when we chew and salivary enzymes start working on our food, but the process then continues in the stomach upon swallowing. In Eastern medicine, which governs the practice of acupuncture, there's a so-called "organ body clock." During a 24-hour period, *qi* (energy) moves in two-hour intervals through the organ systems. When we sleep at night, the energy draws inward to restore the body. Before dawn, it prepares to move outward again, with the liver taking center stage between 1 and 3 AM during deep sleep to detox the blood and prepare the body for waking hours of activity.

As you can likely guess, the stomach's primary time of activity is in the morning, between 7 and 9 AM. This is when the body best assimilates proteins, so a solid protein meal is a great way to start your day. Stomach "conditions" run the gamut, from allergies to ulcers. One of the common causes of allergies is poor protein digestion. Dr. Goodheart often described how when stomach acid is low, proteins are not thoroughly broken down, which in turn challenges the immune system in the form of an antigen attack, causing it to overreact and trigger allergic reactions. A similar mechanism of undigested protein can also cause joint pain and potentially arthritis. There are other faulty digestive and inflammatory triggers involved as well, but fixing the stomach is the place to start in arthritic conditions.

Bad breath is often a manifestation of poor stomach function. So is burping, which could be another sign of low stomach acid. The bowel is intended to clear after each primary meal. If you're not experiencing regular bowel movements that are easy to push out, that's constipation.   Good stomach function is not only good for the whole body and prevention of headaches, but it's also one of our best preventions against parasites. When the stomach works right, the parasites get killed on contact.

Stomach acid can also creep too high and stir trouble, especially when there's gut permeability. If that protective lining is compromised, then an ulceration of the stomach lining may form.

> *When the stomach is working properly and your stomach acids are at the right levels, potential invaders like parasites are killed quickly so they don't harm you.*

POTENTIAL TRIGGERS OF LEFT-SIDED HEAD PAIN

If an imbalance in stomach acid causes left-sided head pain, then the next question is what can trigger that imbalance. Here are the common offenders:

1. Wheat
2. Antacids
3. Acid blocker and proton pump inhibitor medications
4. Some perfumes
5. Poor stress tolerance
6. Emotional challenges of being overly sympathetic, having low self-esteem, or being easily disgusted
7. Nutrient deficiencies of B1, zinc, or calcium

The connection between wheat consumption and low stomach acid may not seem obvious, but I believe there are three chief mechanisms at play here:

1. The poorly digested wheat grains bind up the hydrochloric acid of the stomach.
2. The toxic metals from pesticides in the wheat grains block the formation of hydrochloric acid. Cadmium and arsenic are two toxic metals commonly found in grains and inorganic foods.
3. Natural vitamin B1 (thiamine) is lost during grain processing. When grain processing first became industrialized, there was an increase in thiamine deficiency disease, called beriberi, which is serious and sometimes fatal. Once we figured this out, humans began spraying back in a synthetic source of thiamine called thiamine hydrochloride, which helped decrease the incidence of beriberi, but the artificial form is not

as beneficial as thiamine found in nature (thiamine diphosphate and thiamine triphosphate). When you buy processed grains, cereals, flours, and breads, you'll often see on the labels "enriched with B vitamins."

> *Grains lose most of their natural thiamine (vitamin B1) when processed. Food manufacturers will replace the lost thiamine with a synthetic form. This is how foods become "fortified" or "enriched," but natural thiamine is superior to its synthetic counterpart.*

Many medications inhibit stomach acid. With stomach and reflux problems being extremely prevalent, there is a big market for acid-blocking or acid-inhibiting medications (for therapies associated with reflux/GERD/heartburn problems, see the section on gallbladder and right-sided headaches on page 70). These may give some initial relief, maybe, but they certainly have long-term consequences.

To digest and utilize calcium, we need hydrochloric acid in the stomach. To form hydrochloric acid, we need calcium, and thus goes the vicious cycle of hydrochloric acid deficiency and potential bone compromise. When hydrochloric acid is low or blocked, then calcium metabolism is undermined. This in turn jeopardizes bone health. Another common outcome of long-term acid-blocking medications is autoimmune conditions. When the stomach acid is deficient, causing the poor breakdown of proteins, the immune system can be triggered to attack the body's own tissues (thus, autoimmune conditions ensue). The better solution would be to correct stomach function and avoid the use of acid-compromising medications.

> *Acid-blocking medications, such as the popular proton pump inhibitors (PPIs) Nexium, Prevacid, and Prilosec, are easy to obtain over the counter, but they come with a higher risk of infections, autoimmune disorders, and loss of bone mass and strength.*

Organic vegetables are loaded with more minerals than inorganic vegetables because organic produce comes from healthy, mineral-rich soils. Minerals help form the needed hydrochloric acid and help alkalize the system. An alkaline system digests and resists infections better, is calmer and more emotionally resilient, and supports stronger bones. Sugar and processed foods, on the other hand, acidify the system, and sugar, as you know, will further leach the thiamine necessary for hydrochloric acid. An acidic system is more prone to illness and inflammation, is uptight/ stressed, and is vulnerable to loss of bone strength. Put simply, sugar and processed foods compromise stomach function, while vegetables help maintain it.

> *Minerals from organic vegetables will help alkalize your system to support healthy digestion, resist infections better, boost bone strength, and render you calmer and more emotionally resilient.*

As you start reducing the sugary foods in your diet, the cravings for them will also reduce. When you have cravings for sweets, try eating vegetables or protein with healthy fat. This will help to stabilize your blood sugar and prevent the next irresistible craving. Also, recall that sugar feeds yeast, which then perpetuates the sugar cravings.

> *Yeast love their sugar. When you succumb to a powerful sugar craving, you're feeding that yeast and setting yourself up for an unhealthy overgrowth.*

If you have had sugar cravings, you may also need to take an anti-yeast supplement. Pau d'arco and caprylic acid are popular anti-yeast herbs. Your friends will appreciate the new happier you. Your bones, your scale, your waistline, your digestion, and your hormones will thank you too.

CHAPTER 5

RIGHT-SIDED HEADACHES

Problem in the Gallbladder

In my experience, right-sided headaches are among the most common headaches and are often called "migraines" by sufferers. As I've already mentioned, right-sided headaches are caused by gallbladder dysfunction. Again, check all the boxes that apply to you.

Common Symptoms, Signs, and/or Characteristics Associated with Right-Sided Headaches

☐ *Pain on the right side of your head*
☐ *Pain behind the right or left knee*
☐ *Right ear pain*
☐ *Right shoulder pain or weakness*
☐ *Pain between the shoulders (T4)*
☐ *Right jaw pain*
☐ *Pain in the thumb*
☐ *Bags under the eyes*
☐ *Dry skin*

- ☐ *"Runner's cramp" or "stitch" pain under the right rib cage with activity*
- ☐ *Symptoms worse between 11 PM and 1 AM*
- ☐ *Hiatal hernia*
- ☐ *Sluggish bowel movements (less than one bowel movement a day)*
- ☐ *Left-sided sinus congestion*
- ☐ *Gallbladder removed*
- ☐ *High cholesterol*
- ☐ *Heartburn*
- ☐ *Anxiety*
- ☐ *Frustration*
- ☐ *Resentment*
- ☐ *Pressure in the chest*
- ☐ *Poor memory / recall*
- ☐ *Frequent alcohol consumption*
- ☐ *Trouble falling asleep*
- ☐ *Nausea*
- ☐ *Intolerance to fatty foods*

COULD YOU DIGEST FATS BETTER?

The gallbladder is a right-sided organ, a small sack tucked under and attached to the liver. The two organs work together, as the liver cleanses the blood and then puts those toxins with bile into the gallbladder to be released into the small intestine for elimination. The gallbladder contracts and squirts the bile into the small intestine when fat is sensed there. Therefore, consuming healthy fats is part of keeping the gallbladder cleansed and healthy. Dietary toxins, fried foods, and processed trans fats muck up the gallbladder. The gallbladder's relationship with fat means that when the organ is congested, fat metabolism gets compromised, and poor fat metabolism may lead to intestinal spasms, dry skin, elevated cholesterol, and a weakened immune system.

There is a mechanism called the "ileal brake" in which the valves in the final part of the small intestine (an area called the ileum) clamp down to give the body more time to digest and absorb more nutrients, especially much-needed fat. Its receptors, in fact, respond to the fatty food and send out signals to slow down the movement of that food through the gut. Like a form of gut traffic control, the ileal brake is our gut's natural braking system to absorb more of the fat our bodies require to make hormones, stabilize blood sugar, and keep inflammation down. This action also has the beneficial effect of helping us feel full so we stop eating. The ileal brake was only discovered in the 1980s and has since become a target for appetite control.

Clearly, a balance must be struck because if this brake is overly activated, it can cause lower abdominal pain and/or sluggish bowels. But for the most part, this important speed bump ensures we absorb critical nutrients—particularly those healthy fats. Lack of good fat can lead to dry skin, especially on the heels, and may cause dark circles under the eyes. And because fat is necessary to manufacture certain hormones, like cholesterol, a dietary fat deficiency can trigger the body to compensate by overproducing cholesterol. If you have already made a conscious effort to add quality omega-3 fats to your diet, you probably have added some great quality to your years.

> *Got high cholesterol? While you might want to blame your genetics, you might also want to take a look at your dietary fat intake. You might not be consuming enough dietary cholesterol and your body is in overdrive to make more cholesterol to compensate for the deficiency. Note too that saturated and trans fats have the power to raise blood cholesterol levels more so than dietary cholesterol.*

As Dr. Goodheart began correlating muscles to organ function, he found that the right popliteus muscle, which is a small but major stabilizing muscle in the knee joint, would show weakness with gallbladder problems. He documented that low gallbladder function correlates with an unstable knee that can even lead to ACL tears. The popliteus muscle prevents the knee from hyperextending backwards or over-rotating. This can also be the cause of a Baker's cyst behind the knee. As it's a right-sided organ, I used Goodheart's findings to correlate that gallbladder symptoms predominantly show up on the right side, as in the jaw, knee, foot, or eye, including the right-sided headaches being discussed.

GALLBLADDER IS ON THE RIGHT

By studying the pattern of the gallbladder acupuncture meridian, I determined the right-sided head pain pattern, as well as the right ear pain and right eye problems. This meridian starts at the outer corner of the eye and progresses down through the back of the knee, ending between the fourth and fifth toes. When I was in chiropractic college in the early '90s, it was generally understood that the profile for a gallbladder problem was "fat, female, fertile, and forties." That was also the decade when glyphosate-rich pesticides became more and more prevalent. Glyphosate inhibits bile production, thereby causing gallbladder congestion.[1] This explains why wheat consumption can be problematic. It's no wonder that gallbladder problems are rampant, as are right-sided headaches. In fact, you may be reading this and have already had your gallbladder removed (see page 133 for health advice in this scenario).

> Wheat Woes: One of the most common sources of glyphosate exposure is through wheat and wheat products. Not only is this popular herbicide a potential carcinogen, but its effects on the gallbladder and liver up the risk for organ dysfunction and, in turn, right-sided headaches.

THERE'S A CORRELATION BETWEEN HEADACHES AND MEMORY LOSS

It helps to understand that there's a brain chemical (neurotransmitter) called acetylcholine that drives the gallbladder meridian and regulates gallbladder function. Acetylcholine is a jack of many trades in the body as a key messenger, transferring signals between certain cells that affect an array of bodily functions. In the brain, acetylcholine serves an important role in learning, memory, and recall. It also plays a role in attention and arousal. Elsewhere in the body, it stimulates muscle contractions and helps regulate the heart and blood pressure. Too much or too little of this chemical leads to problems. When it's low, you can have issues with recalling names and information—the "it's on the tip of my tongue" moment. When it's too high, a rarer occurrence, you can have severe muscle contractions, paralysis, and panic attacks. Newer research also shows that anxiety and depression are common in people with gastroesophageal reflux disease (GERD). Up to one in three individuals with GERD experience anxiety and depression. In 2023, the *American Journal of Gastroenterology* published a large review paper covering 36 studies that shined a bright light on a link between GERD and anxiety and depression: "Researchers found that anxiety and depressive symptoms were more than twice as likely in patients with GERD than in healthy controls. Among individuals with GERD, up to one-third and one-fourth were affected by anxiety and depressive symptoms, respectively."[2] I wish they would have also asked about right-sided headaches.

Acetylcholine is an important chemical messenger with many physiological functions throughout the body. It is the most common neurotransmitter and was the first one discovered.

> *In the brain, acetylcholine serves a critical role in learning, memory, and recall.*

In the body, it stimulates muscle contractions and helps regulate the heart and blood pressure. When there's not enough, high blood pressure can be the result. Imbalances of this key chemical have long been implicated in many neurologic conditions, as people with Alzheimer's or Parkinson's disease tend to have low levels. And when it's too high, other problems can ensue, from headaches and confusion to convulsions and death.

Acetylcholine happens to be a precursor molecule to nitric oxide, which is a critical compound made by the body and required for health. Nitric oxide promotes the dilation of blood vessels (what's called a vasodilator); it signals the blood vessels to relax so they can expand and support blood flow to move nutrients and oxygen. Hence, low acetylcholine can lead to low nitric oxide and, in turn, elevated blood pressure. Right-sided headaches could be an early warning for this cardiovascular problem brewing.

> *The gallbladder is among the unsung heroes of your immune system. You can in fact think of your gallbladder as an immune organ. Recent studies have proven that bile acids promote the activity of T cells that are involved in controlling inflammation. Studies also show that gut microbes are key for converting bile acids into immune-signaling molecules.[4]*

The gallbladder does more than assist with fat metabolism and nitric oxide production; turns out it's also associated with building your immune system. When the organ releases bile to digest fats, it secretes immune cells too. These cells prompt the immune system to go to work, with some cells acting as antibacterial agents. In other words, fats essentially initiate both the first responder part of the immune system and the part that is designed to recognize and attack previous bugs. As such, the gallbladder is acutely involved in immune regulation. So when we eat good fats, these immune signals get released into the potentially toxic environment of the intestine. This means right-sided headaches may be an early warning that the immune system is under-functioning.

POTENTIAL TRIGGERS OF RIGHT-SIDED HEAD PAIN

Dallas, a woman in her late 60s, came to me with extreme abdominal pain and nausea, right-sided head pains, and knee and foot pains. Because of the serious pain, Dallas was dependent on her sister to bring her in for this visit. I immediately identified the gallbladder as the principal source of all her pain and nausea, which I attributed to some kind of toxic overload that was compromising her gallbladder's functionality.

Although I recommended she start a simple supplement regimen that would support her gallbladder naturally, the sister, a nurse, felt that Dallas needed to go to the hospital. Against Dallas's better judgment, she checked into the hospital, where she remained for the next two weeks. After many tests and medications, she was released with no answers and the same pain. Back home again, Dallas finally took the supplement I had given her. Within 30 minutes, all her pain, right-sided headaches, and nausea were gone!

Got oat milk? Plant-based alternatives to traditional cow's milk have been all the rage lately. But at what cost? Turns out many of the most popular oat milks on the market contain glyphosate, and not many are certified organic. Non-organic oats contain the highest amount of pesticide residue of any crop in the U.S.! So be careful when choosing your "milk." To find glyphosate residue-free-certified products, check out The Detox Project at www.detoxproject.org.

When my wife started having regular right-sided headaches, she took stock of her lifestyle to find the culprit. She is generally very clean in her dietary choices, but a quick look at her habits showed that oat milk in her daily green tea drink was likely exposing her to glyphosate. Her headaches vanished once she evicted the beverage and found a safer glyphosate-free alternative. The solutions are often that simple and profound when the proper trigger is identified. Here are some of the other common triggers:

1. Low-fat diet (causing fat deficiency)
2. Trans fats
3. Toxic overload
4. Toxic metals
5. Parasites

SOME FATS MAY TAKE MONTHS TO DIGEST

You've probably heard about trans fats, a form of processed fat that's not good for us but that can be found in lots of foods. When food manufacturers want to produce products with longer shelf lives, they want to avoid fats turning rancid, so they will heat the good, unsaturated oils to give them that longer shelf life. The bad news for us as consumers is that these heated trans fats are not readily recognized by the digestive tract and can take a long time to metabolize. Yes, that means that the French fries you ate yesterday may still be mucking up your system months from now. Even though people are more aware of trans fats and labels must indicate the presence of these fats, they still lurk, and you may not be paying attention when you consume them. In the program, you'll learn how to automatically avoid trans fats and give your gallbladder a fighting chance to be as healthy as possible.

> *According to our finest healthcare establishments, from the Mayo Clinic to the National Institutes of Health, your body needs ZERO trans fats. Your body does not need or benefit from these fats commonly found in fried and battered foods, shortening and stick margarine, and many packaged or processed foods, including commercially baked goods (e.g., cakes, pies, cookies). The body doesn't process these fats easily, so they can have lasting effects long after you eat them.*

PARASITES ARE PREVALENT

Parasites are a health thief, and they are far more common than you might suspect. When I look at potential sources, approximately 70 percent of the carriers include pets, so make sure to keep them healthy and clean at all times. Other common sources include foods like sushi and lettuce. These are less risky when stomach acid is adequate to digest the parasites upon consumption. A common place for parasites to linger is in the liver, corrupting bile production. Killing them with herbs like wormwood and oregano can be helpful for optimum liver and gallbladder function.

Finally, before we move on to the next type of pain, I want to explain why eating bread and tomatoes can trigger right-sided headaches. If bread is made from glyphosate-tainted grains, there's your hit to the gallbladder. Tomatoes can inhibit acetylcholine in some people, notably those with blood type A and B. As you know now, a deficiency in acetylcholine will have a host of downstream effects, from gallbladder congestion to poor memory recall, reduced nitric oxide, and increased blood pressure. I challenge you: How much better would you feel if you reduced foods with tomato, wheat, and trans fats? And even better if you added more fish oil?

CHAPTER 6

BACK-HEAD PAIN ("TENSION HEADACHES")

Problem in the Thyroid

I s there a parallel trend in the rise of thyroid conditions and the prevalence of back-of-the-head "tension" headaches? I think so. The numbers speak for themselves. According to the American Thyroid Association:[1]

- More than 12 percent of the U.S. population will develop a thyroid condition during their lifetime, with women more likely than men to have thyroid problems.
- An estimated 20 million Americans have some form of thyroid disease, but upwards of 60 percent of those people don't know it.
- Undiagnosed thyroid disease may put patients at risk for certain serious conditions, such as heart issues and cardiovascular diseases, osteoporosis, depression, slow cognition and poor memory, and infertility.
- "The causes of thyroid problems are largely unknown."

That last fact is astonishing when you think about it. How can we not know what triggers the thyroid to misbehave in our modern world of medicine? Before we have that conversation, let's get to know this vitally important master gland that produces hormones to influence almost all of the metabolic processes in the body.

Butterfly in shape and located at the base of the neck, the thyroid commands the production of hormones that regulate metabolism, helps control protein synthesis, and adjusts the body's sensitivity to other hormones. It is also involved in growth functions, immunity, cognition, and detoxification. When it underperforms and doesn't produce enough of certain key hormones, that's hypothyroidism. Symptoms include fatigue, constipation, hair loss, low mood and depression, foggy thinking, feeling cold all the time, low metabolism, weight gain, dry skin, muscle aches, and an intolerance for exercise.

Common Symptoms, Signs, and/or Characteristics Associated with Back-Head Pain

- ☐ *Pain in the back of the head*
- ☐ *Pain in the center of the lower back (L5)*
- ☐ *Pain in the side of the neck*
- ☐ *Weakness in the back of the neck*
- ☐ *Weight gain*
- ☐ *Bloating*
- ☐ *Sluggish metabolism*
- ☐ *Hair loss*
- ☐ *Dry skin*
- ☐ *Hypothyroidism*
- ☐ *Loss of hair at the outer third of eyebrow*
- ☐ *Clear sinus drainage*
- ☐ *Cold hands and/or feet*

□ *Depression*
□ *Overly emotional state, tearfulness*
□ *Erratic menstrual cycles*
□ *Infertility*
□ *Sluggish digestion (one or fewer bowel movements a day)*
□ *Low TSH (hyperthyroidism)*
□ *Low energy*
□ *Weak gluteal muscles*
□ *Adrenal fatigue*
□ *Seasonal depression*
□ *Lower back disc problem*

A Master Gland: The thyroid is among the most important hormonal glands, releasing certain hormones that affect virtually every cell in your body. Through its actions, the thyroid controls the speed of your metabolism, helps manage how much protein your body makes, regulates body temperature, and calibrates the body's sensitivity to other hormones. It ultimately affects everything about you—from how your body uses energy to your heart rate, breathing, digestion, weight, and moods.

Hypothyroidism is incredibly common today, especially among women. By some estimates, upward of 20 percent of all women have a so-called "lazy" thyroid. Synthroid, the drug used to mimic the natural thyroid hormone your body makes, is one of the most prescribed medications in America today. On the other hand, when the gland is overactive and producing too much thyroid hormone, a condition called *hyper*thyroidism sets in, which has its own basket of symptoms—from irritability, mood swings, and fatigue to muscle weakness, trouble sleeping, irregular heartbeat, and diarrhea.

Specifically, the thyroid is responsible for producing what's called T0, T1, T2, T3, and T4. The first three are hormone precursors and by-products of making thyroid hormone; the most active and talked-about hormones are T3 and T4, the latter of which is the storage form of thyroid hormone (called thyroxine) that gets converted into its active T3 form. The conversion process depends on specialized enzymes, optimal cortisol levels, and certain nutrients such as iron, iodine, zinc, magnesium, selenium, B vitamins, vitamin C, and vitamin D. Hence, if there's a deficiency in any of these "ingredients," your thyroid will suffer. What's more, many exposures we encounter daily can interfere with thyroid function, from commercial food products and plastics that contain thyroid-disrupting chemicals to fluoride-filled tap water and mercury-laden fish.

> *Numerous exposures in our environment can impact healthy thyroid function. Examples of thyroid disruptors include the synthetic chemicals and bioactive compounds found in food, air, water, and products we use daily. Many of these disruptors are insidious for their ability to mimic the thyroid's structure, invade the gland, and cause damage.*

I should reiterate that thyroid health is so much more than pumping out hormonal products. Thyroid health involves a sophisticated conversation between the gland, the brain, hormones, and the receiving cells and tissues. Like that intricate web, there are many layers to the healthy functioning of *anything* in the body. Just as the thyroid can be ground zero for problems that manifest in a variety of conditions—headaches being among them—dysfunctions elsewhere in the body can also lead to direct and indirect influences on thyroid health.

As with many of the headaches discussed in this book, scientific research has not yet adequately described the exact mechanism of how the thyroid refers pain to the back of the head. However, based on my experience and a look at studies in motion today, some of which are in clinical trials, I can confidently propose that there's a connection between thyroid activity and the muscles in the back of the neck. When the enzymes needed to convert T4 to T3 are not adequate, it causes the muscles in the back of the neck and attached to the base of the skull to be weak. Such weakness results in the tension headache pattern. It also can cause a reduction in the neck's range of motion in both rotation and side bending (when you feel like you need to stretch your neck, there could be a thyroid problem looming).

> *Signs of thyroid problems can show up on your skin, in your hair, on your nails, and even in how your neck feels. If you feel the urge to stretch your neck because it's tight or there's a sensation that food is stuck in the throat, that could be indicative of a thyroid problem.*

In 1994, I wrote an observational paper for the International College of Applied Kinesiology in which I described the link between weakness of those neck muscles and weakness in the lower back that sets the stage for lower back pain and potential lumbar disc problems. People diagnosed with Hashimoto's disease, an autoimmune condition characterized by an attack on the thyroid from the body's own immune system, are often documented to have back and disc problems. I see this frequently in my practice, and it's a classic domino effect. The attack does more than hit the thyroid; it causes the top three cervical vertebrae to "fixate," or move as one unit. This fixation causes both gluteus maximus muscles to weaken, which creates significant pressure on the lowest disc (L5-S1) in the back. Left untreated, the condition can eventually lead to disc problems. Again, recall that web analogy: you disturb one area, you disturb other areas as a consequence.

> *The surprising connection between the thyroid and your back: If your thyroid is under attack, it can actually lead to back issues and disc problems through a well-defined cascade of effects.*

I liken optimum thyroid function to upgrading a processing chip. As we'll see in Part III, there are ways to support a healthy thyroid without the drug route. I have resolved many patients' thyroid issues through supplementation that boosts the conversion of the inactive T4 to the active T3. This requires certain enzymes, nutrients, and minerals to be at the ready.

Sometimes it's just one missing ingredient that needs to be filled, as illustrated by my patient Paul. When I first met Paul, he had been to the emergency room four weeks prior for the pain in the left side of his head and neck that radiated down his left arm. This is an ominous symptom that will get you to the front of the line in any medical facility due to the significant cardiovascular risk it represents. The result of that ER visit was "No aneurysm."

Paul had a history of hypothyroidism, hyperthyroidism, and low testosterone. At the time of his first visit with me, he was taking testosterone and the anti-thyroid drug methimazole for hyperthyroidism. The methimazole, however, came with disruptive side effects. Paul had flu-like symptoms, extreme fatigue between 12 and 3 PM and again from 8 to 9 PM, and he felt like he had pins and needles in both arms. Methimazole lists headaches, numbness/tingling, and muscle and joint pains as potential side effects, so this was not surprising.

My initial exam determined that he was low in zinc and showed signs of adrenal fatigue, noted by the fact his pupil constricted for only 1.36 seconds when light was shined into his eye; it should stay constricted for at least 24 seconds when the body is properly handling stress. I felt weaknesses and spasms in muscles linked to the thyroid, and signs of an autoimmune attack against his thyroid were also present. The fact that his body temperature was on the cooler side (96.3°F) further confirmed a dysfunctional thyroid, as this gland is pivotal in regulating the body's temperature.

The common thread for virtually all of Paul's symptoms and exam findings was clear as day for me: a need for vitamin B1 (thiamine). Functionally, thiamine helps the thyroid produce thyroxine (T4), helps nerve transmission, helps break down and make testosterone, helps the heart contract more efficiently, helps calcium get into the bones, and helps maintain tone in the veins. Thiamine also helps the stomach make the hydrochloric acid it needs to break foods down. It can help the pupil maintain constriction to block bright lights and be able to focus far away.

In addition to "prescribing" a B-vitamin formulation with higher levels of thiamine, I also recommended Paul significantly reduce grains, especially whole wheat. As already discussed, processed flours and white rice are well known to create a deficiency of thiamine. What's more, part of the whole wheat's amino acid sequence resembles the thyroid gland's amino acid sequence.

This is precisely how an incoming ingredient as seemingly innocuous as whole wheat can trigger a self-inflicted attack on the gland. It's called molecular mimicry. When the immune system identifies an irritant—in this case, whole wheat—it begins producing antibodies against it. These antibodies can then misidentify the thyroid as "non-self" and launch an autoimmune attack against the gland. This mechanism is far more prevalent when the intestinal barrier is compromised.

When Paul returned for his follow-up visit about four weeks later, he had not experienced any headaches and his energy and motivation were much better. Most of the symptoms had resolved, and he no longer showed signs of an autoimmune reaction against his thyroid. At that time, we reduced his supplement dosage and added a zinc supplement. He could not be happier!

Interestingly, one telltale sign of a simple thiamine deficiency that leaves the thyroid underperforming is being a mosquito magnet. I once treated a nine-year-old girl for daily headaches in both temples. A thiamine deficiency can trigger both temple and back-head tension headaches. As I evaluated the girl, I noticed scars on her arms from old bug bites. Her father quickly chimed in, "Mosquitoes love my daughter"—a key piece of information.

> *Mosquito magnet? Check your thyroid. You might have*
> *a thiamine deficiency that renders you attractive to*
> *the bugs because you can't metabolize aldehydes. As*
> *aldehydes build up, you give off a fruity, "come-bite-me"*
> *smell. Boost your thiamine levels, kill the scent, and stop*
> *the bug bites.*

Mosquitoes are attracted to people who are deficient in thiamine because when there is a thiamine deficiency, the body does not metabolize aldehydes properly. Aldehydes are organic compounds found throughout the environment and in foods you ingest. Without proper metabolism of aldehydes, a person can give off a fruity smell that the bugs can detect (aldehydes also happen to be used a lot in the perfumery business). Not only did I detect that the girl's thyroid deficiency was fueling her headaches, but I also suspected that the deficiency was further impacting her body's ability to metabolize estrogen—a hormone that depends on thiamine to control its balance so there's not too much circulating in the system. Excess estrogen can precipitate headaches. No sooner did we start the girl on a vitamin B1–rich supplement than her headaches resolved and the mosquitoes found someone else to bite.

Could you use some improvement in mental processing? Could your mood be better? Any hair loss or weight gain? If you reduced thyroid-disrupting exposures and wheat consumption and increased intake of organic vegetables, how much better would you feel? You may even further benefit from taking a thiamine supplement.

POTENTIAL TRIGGERS OF BACK-HEAD PAIN

The thyroid receives feedback from many other glands, which makes it very vulnerable to imbalances. Some common culprits of creating an imbalance include the following:

1. Exposure to toxic metals, synthetic chemicals, and other bioactive compounds and contaminants like fluoride that can impair thyroid function
2. Too many processed foods and refined flours and grains (e.g., wheat)
3. Poor blood sugar control
4. Poor stress tolerance
5. Deficiencies in iodine or thiamine
6. Estrogen imbalance (hence, women are more affected by thyroid issues)

CHAPTER 7

FRONTAL (FOREHEAD) HEADACHES

Problem with Stomach Lining

It's the classic image of a headache sufferer—the person taking a stress break from work at a desk to rest their forehead into a hand, comforting emanating pain. Frontal headaches share something in common with left-sided headaches: a problem in the stomach largely due to stress. But with frontal headaches, the core trigger has to do with too much *chronic* stress, which has rippling effects that ultimately impact the stomach's lining. By chronic, I am not referring to the occasional stressful moment when you're avoiding an accident or having an isolated bad day at work. I'm referring to the kind of stress that's pervasive and relentless and that hangs like a dark cloud over your entire day.

I'd like to share a true story that demonstrates how changes in digestion and detoxification can have profoundly positive effects on one's life, especially one's outlook and relationships. Jennifer was at odds with her husband and children when she came to see me. She'd gone to the elders at her church and received "biblical grounds for divorce." When she returned one month later after we started her on herbs to support her digestive system and her liver's ability to break down stress hormones, she gave me a massive hug and stated, "I love my husband and children again!" Now that's a story worth passing along.

Common Symptoms, Signs, and / or Characteristics
Associated with Frontal Headaches

- ☐ *Pain in the front of the head*
- ☐ *Pain below the shoulder blades*
- ☐ *Anxiety*
- ☐ *Depression*
- ☐ *Trouble falling asleep*
- ☐ *Burning in the stomach area*
- ☐ *History of ulcers*
- ☐ *History of H. pylori infections*
- ☐ *Elevated blood pressure*
- ☐ *Weak ankles*
- ☐ *Reverse T3 in your thyroid panel*
- ☐ *Frequent caffeine consumption*
- ☐ *Obsessive behavior*
- ☐ *Blood sugar dips*
- ☐ *Stress-triggered illness*

THIS HEADACHE *IS* CAUSED BY STRESS

Chronic stress can compromise the stomach lining (think ulcers). Stress-induced disruption to the stomach's lining happens when important biochemicals become imbalanced. Key messengers like serotonin and noradrenaline normally protect the stomach lining and become deficient under chronic stress. Farther down your gastrointestinal (GI) tract, in your intestines, that stress can also impact the intestinal lining. When it becomes "leaky," as we've discussed, trouble looms. Intestinal permeability is associated with a slew of health challenges, as molecules meant to stay in the gut can find their way on the other side and incite, among other things, pain-inducing inflammation that manifests as a headache.

Certain neurotransmitters are important for proper digestive activity, especially in the stomach, where food is broken down into smaller bits to be moved on for nutrient absorption in the intestines. One of the key neurotransmitters is noradrenaline, also called norepinephrine, which doubles as a hormone. To be clear: noradrenaline and adrenaline are not the same. Adrenaline is purely a hormone, whereas noradrenaline is both a hormone and neurotransmitter—it can travel through the bloodstream as well as across neural pathways.

Noradrenaline is produced mostly by the adrenal glands but also in the brain stem. We often think of norepinephrine as our "fight-or-flight" hormone. Indeed, in the brain, it primes us for battle by triggering wakefulness and attention. But it's not just released upon signs of danger; it's released normally throughout the day when you need to be more alert. It's how you get out of bed in the morning, as your brain sends a burst of noradrenaline into your bloodstream. If you've ever felt a burst of energy after feeling depleted during a hard workout, you can thank noradrenaline for that. Low amounts of noradrenaline are, in fact, coursing through your central nervous system to assist and regulate basic bodily functions. When you encounter stress or an existential threat, however, more is pumped out to prepare you for action.

Noradrenaline wears many hats. This hormone that doubles as a neurotransmitter is uniquely tied to stress reactions and affects the areas of the brain that are responsible for controlling attention, concentration, and action. It's connected to the fight-or-flight response: it can increase the heart rate, release glucose from energy stores, and boost blood flow to skeletal muscles. At low levels, noradrenaline is associated with major depressive disorder, and at high levels, it can have adverse effects on the heart and circulatory system, contribute to high blood pressure, trigger severe headaches, and even damage the kidneys.

While noradrenaline awakens the brain, it has different effects outside the brain, where it constricts blood vessels, raises blood pressure, increases heart rate, and, as a result, causes a decrease in blood flow to the gastrointestinal tract.[1] Norepinephrine inhibits the intestinal nervous system, which in turn means decreased digestive activity, including less secretion of digestive enzymes needed for proper digestion. When your body senses danger and puts you in alert mode to flee or fight a potential hazard, you don't want your body's energy going to activity in the digestive system. Instead, you want your energy focused in your brain for thinking, making quick decisions, and producing memories of the event for future reference. Digestion is a nonessential function when you're in danger, but chronic activation of the fight-or-flight pathway that keeps digestion suppressed will lead to trouble—trouble that can manifest in frontal headaches. In addition to prolonged exposure to chronic stress pushing levels of norepinephrine below normal due to the underactivity of the stress response system, chronic stress can prevent norepinephrine's important role in *protecting* the stomach lining. As the balance of norepinephrine goes awry under chronic stress, the stomach lining suffers and becomes vulnerable to injury, which in turn causes frontal headaches.

DOES YOUR HEAD "FEEL GOOD"?

Serotonin is another critical neurotransmitter. The "feel-good" brain chemical is famously targeted by popular SSRI antidepressants that are supposed to increase the availability of this chemical in the brain. Selective serotonin reuptake inhibitors (SSRIs) are a class of drugs used to treat depression. Most people don't realize that the majority of the body's serotonin, however, is not made in the brain: 95 percent of it is manufactured in the gut's nerve cells within the gut wall with the help of gut microbes and the raw materials they create. This is partly why scientists call the gut our "second brain."[2] It houses innumerable neurons and even more innumerable beneficial microbes.

When antidepressants fail, the new thinking is that perhaps trying to raise levels of serotonin in the brain is not nearly as effective as nourishing a healthy gut to support a healthy balance of this chemical. To be clear, the term "gut" technically refers to the entire GI system that goes from the beginning of the esophagus to the anus. Even though people tend to use the term to speak squarely about the intestines, it's used in scientific circles to describe the "gut-brain axis," in which a network of communication happens with the help of neurotransmitters. These neurotransmitters regulate the entire GI system and have a unique ability to speak to the brain from "the gut."

> *The vast majority of the body's serotonin—fully 95 percent—is manufactured in the gut with the help of nearby microbes. Trillions of microbes line the gut and lord over a wide range of activities—digestion, metabolism, immunity, inflammation, memory, mood, learning, pain perception, and more.*

The idea that the microbes in our GI system, our microbiome, command and control a lot of our functionality is taking the medical world by storm as scientists decipher its mysteries. Its highly sophisticated neural network can continue to work on its own even after the vagus nerve—the primary neural highway between the enteric nervous system and the brain—is severed. The gut's nervous system works in collaboration with the enveloping microbiome too.

HAPPINESS STARTS IN THE GUT

Our intestinal environments, dominated by bacteria, also include other microbes that develop largely after birth over time and in response to a variety of factors, from genetics to environment, including dietary inputs. Over 100 trillion microbes line the gut and lord over a wide range of activities—digestion, metabolism, immunity, inflammation, memory, mood, learning, pain perception…the list goes on. In addition to serotonin, they can produce and respond to norepinephrine, dopamine, acetylcholine, melatonin, and GABA, the latter of which is an important neurotransmitter that keeps anxiety in check. Note that these are all the same neurochemicals our brains use to regulate our mood and cognition.

In one of the earliest studies published in 1998, microbiologist Mark Lyte, then at Texas Tech University Health Sciences Center, fed a small dose of a pathogenic bacteria (*Campylobacter jejuni*) to a group of mice.[3] The dose was too tiny to stir an immune response, but enough to trigger behavioral changes through the shift in the microbial balance. Two days after the mice were exposed to the bad bacteria, they acted more cautiously compared with the control mice not given the bacteria. The intestinal environment's role in mood and anxiety disorders in particular has been rewriting the playbooks for mental health advocates and the entire field of psychiatry.

The delicate dance between our gut's environment and our biology means that any imbalance can impact the amount and actions of important chemical messengers. Too much or too little of these key regulators of many biological functions can lead to gut dysfunction and, ultimately, headaches. Low serotonin, for instance, is classically linked to depression, whereas high serotonin is associated with anxiety and, at the extreme, obsessive-compulsive disorder (OCD). I should temper that statement, however, with the fact that sometimes low serotonin can also be linked with OCD and anxiety disorders.

> *The lows and highs of serotonin: Too little of this influencial neurotransmitter and you'll be at risk for depression; too much and you'll be restless, confused, and anxious.*

Even though depression and anxiety are often lumped together because you can suffer from both, there's a subtle difference. Anxiety entails nervous thoughts, fear, and exaggerated worries about the future. Depression involves a profound sense of hopelessness. The two conditions, however, do share a lot of symptoms in common. They both are fueled by pervasive negative thinking and can manifest in physical pain, digestive issues, nausea, and, of course, headaches. They also promote systemic inflammation, an overactive stress response, and insults to the GI tract's lining.

Whenever I treat a patient with frontal headaches and they also complain of anxiety, I often recommend supplements that contain adaptogenic herbs and compounds used for stress and nervous system support. Of course, the priority in preventing frontal headaches in the first place should be to nurture your microbiome and avoid any compromise to both the lining of the stomach and the intestines. Breakdowns of that mucosal lining of the stomach open the door for highly acidic stomach acid to damage the protective barrier. Those breakdowns are correlated to poor handling of psychological stress and its downstream effects on levels of hormones, neurotransmitters, and other biochemicals necessary for total headache-free wellness.

> *Nurturing your microbiome and protecting the lining of the stomach and intestines will go a long way to prevent frontal headaches.*

THERE IS A CORRELATION BETWEEN HEADACHES AND BAD BREATH

Another culprit to the integrity of your stomach's lining in particular is a bacteria called *Helicobacter pylori* (*H. pylori*). This is a species of bacteria you've likely heard about before, as it's famously linked to peptic ulcers because it can overgrow and burrow its way into the stomach lining, setting the stage for sores. But it also helps with appetite regulation and protects the esophagus, so it's not always the bad guy. Our digestive tracts are no longer filled with as much *H. pylori* as they once were due to antibiotic use and hygienic living conditions. In the words of Dr. Martin Blaser, a celebrated researcher on the microbiome and author of *Missing Microbes*, "...*H. pylori* is really a double-edged sword: as you age, it increases your risk for ulcers and then later for stomach cancer, but it is good for the esophagus, protecting you against GERD and its consequences, including a different cancer. As *H. pylori* is disappearing, stomach cancer is falling, but esophageal adenocarcinoma is rising. It is a classic case of amphibiosis. The facts are consistent."[4] By using the word *amphibiosis*, Dr. Blaser is referring to a term coined decades ago by microbial ecologist Theodor Rosebury. It describes "a relationship between two life forms that is either symbiotic or parasitic, depending on the context—as representative of most relationships between humans and their indigenous organisms."[5]

Fortunately, there are herbs like slippery elm and mastic gum that work very well to "release" *H. pylori* from the lining (see Part III). Then one can rebuild stomach function and reduce symptoms of frontal headaches and digestive distress.

One important takeaway to remember going forward is that the microbiome is incredibly impressionable. Its composition and diversity can shift rather quickly in response to your diet and other habits, from sleep and exercise to your ability to cope with stress. As levels of noradrenaline go up and are sustained by chronic stress, gut function goes down. The release of that noradrenaline in times of stress is not just happening in your adrenals and coursing through your bloodstream; recent research reveals that it can flood the insides of your gut, where "it can directly communicate with your gut microbes," says Dr. Emeran Mayer, a preeminent researcher in the field and the founding director of the Goodman-Luskin Microbiome Center at UCLA.[6] He goes on to write in his best-selling book *The Mind-Gut Connection* that several studies have shown that "norepinephrine can stimulate the growth of bacterial pathogens that can cause serious gut infections, stomach ulcers, and even sepsis. In addition to the growth-promoting ability of this stress molecule, it is also able to activate genes in pathogens, making them more aggressive and increasing their odds of survival in the intestine." What's more, certain gut microbes can even go so far as to chemically change norepinephrine that's present in the gut during stressful periods, such that the molecule is rendered more powerful—"intensifying the effect of the hormone on other microbes."

> *Imbalances of hormones in the gut can stir trouble. Too much norepinephrine, for instance, can promote the growth of bad bacteria that cause infections, stomach ulcers, and even sepsis. Too much estrogen and the digestive system can become acidic and more conducive to yeast overgrowth.*

Suffice to say, we don't want norepinephrine speaking out of line in the body and wreaking havoc in our digestive tract, which eventually manifests as pain elsewhere. I realize that gaining the upper hand on stress in today's world is a feat all on its own, but this program will help you do just that.

POTENTIAL TRIGGERS OF FRONTAL HEAD PAIN

Unrelenting stress is a prime suspect when it comes to frontal headaches. When stress is allowed to simmer to the point it outpaces controls in the system, multiple negative effects occur— frontal headaches being among them, as pain from the stomach refers to the head. As the digestive system struggles, the stomach lining becomes compromised, and the body is forced into a mode that invites dysfunction. Not only do inflammatory pathways spark pain that can manifest in frontal headaches, but the gut dysfunction creates a domino effect with far-reaching repercussions.

To think that frontal headaches are an early warning for risk of peptic ulcers and stomach cancer speaks volumes. In Part III, I'll be giving you a cheat sheet for healing a broken stomach barrier and reclaiming control of your stress response. We all have to deal with stress in our lives, and our bodies are built for it. The secret is to fortify your stress system in ways that keep it in check to ensure that it works for you—not against you. And it could be as simple as adding a *"Reset Day"* to your week and cautiously protecting it.

Previous concussion? I should also note that if you've experienced a concussion in the past that was not properly addressed, that can be a source of chronic stress too. The release of glutamate (as we discussed with monosodium glutamate) is a byproduct of neural degeneration that often occurs long after a concussion. This glutamate keeps the nervous and digestive systems in a state of alarm, which itself is perceived as chronic stress—potentially leading to frontal headaches.

CHAPTER 8

CYCLOPS HEADACHES

Problem in the Pituitary Gland

Thirty-something years old, Debbie ran a successful business and seemingly "had it all together." Yet, she desperately wanted a child. She and her husband had been trying for several years before she flew in to see me. Her story was unique in that she'd had a breast augmentation procedure because she had never developed them during puberty or experienced a normal menstrual cycle. These were clear signs of an underdeveloped pituitary. The telltale symptom was monthly headaches located in the center of her forehead right between the eyes, above the bridge of the nose, or what I call "cyclops" headaches.

Common Symptoms, Signs, and/or Characteristics
Associated with Cyclops Headaches

☐ *Central pain between the eyes (the "third eye")*
☐ *Pain in the center of the lower back*
☐ *Failure to thrive*
☐ *Hypothyroidism*
☐ *Hormonal imbalance*
☐ *Delayed puberty*
☐ *Erratic menstruation*
☐ *Poor recovery*
☐ *Accelerated aging*
☐ *Temperature sensitivity*
☐ *Sluggish digestion*

Debbie's headache pattern is one I've routinely seen among patients with pituitary issues. Think of the pituitary as "air traffic control" for the hormones. Let me give you a general understanding about these key molecules that command so much of our physiology down to how we feel.

Hormones make up our endocrine system and are biological messengers produced in glands such as the pituitary, hypothalamus, thyroid, adrenals, pancreas, ovaries, and testes. Once secreted from their original glands, they travel through the blood to other parts of the body, where they exert their effects. These biological messengers typically act at vanishingly small concentrations and serve many vital roles, from regulating metabolism to growth and development between birth and maturity. There are more than fifty different hormones and related molecules that together control nearly every bodily process and are critical to the function of every tissue and organ. And one of the most important command centers for a wide variety of hormones is your pituitary.

> *Your pituitary gland, the "master gland of the body," produces many essential hormones, such as growth hormone, thyroid-stimulating hormone (TSH), corticotropin (which triggers the adrenals to release cortisol), and vasopressin (which controls water balance and sodium levels).*

The pituitary sits deeply protected in the center of the brain, where it receives feedback from the ovaries or testes, thyroid, and adrenals.[1]   It manipulates hormone production based on what the hormonal needs are and has influence on the rate of digestion. The pituitary is best known for its production of the hormones TSH (thyroid-stimulating hormone) and growth hormone, among others. When you hear the term "failure to thrive," it's usually in reference to children who do not physically develop normally according to standardized growth charts (i.e., height and weight). The reason: their underperforming pituitary fails to supply proper growth hormone. The pituitary is far from a lone soldier, as it works in close harmony with the hypothalamus. Think of the hypothalamus as your thermostat. It ramps up metabolism, thereby causing a fever when the body is fighting a virus. Viruses may incidentally cause damage to either the hypothalamus or the pituitary. The hypothalamus is also referred to as the seat of our emotions because it commands much of our emotional processing.

The moment you feel nervous, anxious, or extremely overwhelmed, the hypothalamus releases a stress coordinator called corticotropin-releasing hormone (CRH) to start a cascade of reactions that ends with cortisol flowing into your bloodstream from the adrenals so you can deal with the stressor. Cortisol is your get-up-and-go hormone that's naturally highest in the early morning, declines throughout the day, and reaches its lowest at midnight. But your adrenals also release excess cortisol when you're anxious or under intense stress. The symphonic relationship between your hypothalamus, pituitary, and adrenals actually has a name: the *HPA axis*, which governs the body's stress response, involving multiple hormones—many of which are released by the pituitary.

> *Viruses can inflict damage to the hypothalamus and pituitary, the latter of which can refer pain to the center of the forehead when it's not working properly. Targeted supplementation, however, can help heal a broken pituitary. See HeadacheAdvantage.com for my recommendations.*

When this critical gland is not functioning properly, pain is typically referred to the center of the forehead, just above the bridge of the nose, in a region that is about two fingers in diameter. When estrogen is compromised, then there can be pain in the hips, at the upper gluteal area, and this ultimately inhibits the pituitary. When the pituitary is not properly regulating the thyroid via TSH, then there may be pain along the front side of the neck (scalene muscle region) or across the lower back at the beltline.

POTENTIAL TRIGGERS OF CYCLOPS HEAD PAIN

Barring congenital or developmental problems that compromise the pituitary's job and performance, several lifestyle triggers can also be at play. Among them are the following:

1. Sugar
2. Improperly administered hormonal birth control or hormone replacement therapy
3. Glyphosate exposure

Sugar, as you already should know, is a master disruptor of hormones in general. And you also know now that I routinely suggest my patients cut back on refined and added sugars, no matter which type of headache they have. But if you have already tackled the "sugar monster," virtually eliminating the refined sugars from your diet, and you still have cyclops headaches, then there may be other triggers, such as hormonal birth control or possibly too much corn consumption and glyphosate exposure. In my experience, the pituitary most commonly simply needs to be healed by targeted supplementation (see Part III).

For Debbie, I determined that she likely had an autoimmune attack against her pituitary, and this adversely affected her thyroid, ovaries, and uterus. I told her to take a single supplement well documented to support the health and function of her pituitary. Six weeks later, she returned to announce a positive pregnancy and no more headaches!

Even though cyclops headaches involve an imbalance of hormones, many of which dominate in females, men are not exempt from this type of headache.

Walter sought my care a bit late in his own saga. By the time I saw him, his left eye was nearly blind and pointing all the way to the left. His right eye was his primary source of vision. He had been having splitting cyclops headaches for several years, and the combination of debilitating headaches, very low energy, and a significant reduction in vision left kindhearted Walter unable to work for nearly a month. His vision was further disturbed because he had a growth on his pituitary that was compressing his optic nerve, which crosses near the pituitary.

I started Walter on the same supplement to support his pituitary gland, and within two days, his headaches were gone. But the growth on his pituitary was substantial and limited his vision. He went through with a surgical procedure to remove part of the gland and was warned he could need long-term treatment with the steroid prednisone and possibly thyroid medication. Luckily, Walter followed my lead and continued the natural supplement regimen to boost his pituitary and adrenal glands. Walter's vision, energy levels, and work production normalized, and he said goodbye to headaches. He's back in the game of life.

CHAPTER 9

PAIN IN THE SIDES OF THE HEAD (TEMPLES)

Problem with Hormone Balance

This should start to sound familiar, as we've already covered some territory in the hormone department. But when it comes to temple headaches, it's imbalances in the male- and female-related hormones—estrogens, progesterone, and testosterone—that cause problems. There are primarily three estrogens that are responsible for the female characteristics and the female cycle. Biochemical pathways in the liver are in place to break these estrogens down when the body is done with them, yet certain environments can inhibit their breakdown. Too much insulin, for instance, can cause excess estrogen.

Common Symptoms, Signs, and/or Characteristics
Associated with Temple Headaches

☐ *Pain in the sides of the head*
☐ *Pain on the outside of the elbow*
☐ *Painful menstruation*
☐ *Pain or inflammation in the middle (third) finger*
☐ *Pain at the outer hip*
☐ *Emotional state*
☐ *Crying during "chick flicks"*
☐ *Unpredictable cycles*
☐ *Weight gain in the hip area (women)*
☐ *Abdominal weight gain (men)*
☐ *Man boobs*
☐ *Lack of motivation*
☐ *Facial hair in women*
☐ *History of ovarian cysts*
☐ *History of endometriosis*
☐ *Breakthrough menstruation*
☐ *Low T3 (thyroid)*
☐ *Sugar cravings*
☐ *Vivid dreams*
☐ *Low or apathetic mood*
☐ *Poor memory storage*
☐ *MTHFR gene mutation*
☐ *Chemical sensitivity*
☐ *Sensitivity to cold*
☐ *Symptoms that flare between 9 and 11 PM*
☐ *Acne, especially in the chin or cheek area*
☐ *Acne on the back*
☐ *Frequent alcohol consumption*

Progesterone, an anti-inflammatory and calming steroid hormone made from cholesterol, builds the lining of the uterus for the start of pregnancy and has a starring role in a woman's cycle after ovulation. But too much stress can dampen its production. Testosterone gives the quintessential male characteristics of drive and facilitates muscle growth and development. Males and females have all three hormones at different proportions. When these hormones are out of balance, then they can manifest as pain in both temples, causing a bitemporal headache.

> *The insulin-estrogen connection in women: When there's too much insulin in the system, the ovaries will produce more testosterone and trigger other hormonal imbalances that lead to excess estrogen.*

The muscles that get tender and weak when the reproductive hormones are out of balance are the gluteus medius, piriformis, and adductor (groin) muscles. When these are functionally compromised, they cause pain in the upper gluteal region. Another area of referred pain when hormones are out of balance is the outside of the elbow, commonly referred to as "tennis elbow." The third (middle) finger is where the acupuncture meridian called *circulation sex* goes and can also be stiff and/or tender when hormones are imbalanced.

The brain controls estrogen via the famous neurotransmitter dopamine. Dopamine can go up with estrogen excess and down with estrogen deficiency. Symptoms of dopamine excess are vivid dreams and, at the extreme, schizophrenia. When dopamine is low, on the other hand, one might experience depression, lack of motivation, and, at the other extreme, Parkinson's. Put simply, poor estrogen metabolism may very well be a precursor to these conditions.

> *Down with dopamine: Low dopamine will put you down in the dumps and raise your risk for Parkinson's. Too much of this mood lifter, however, can promote aggressive behavior and even psychosis.*

A note about the MTHFR gene listed in the checklist: The MTHFR gene provides the instructions for your body to produce the methylenetetrahydrofolate reductase (MTHFR) enzyme, which is essential for several bodily processes. This gene works chiefly by instigating a multistep process that initially converts vitamin B9 (folate) into methylfolate, which is essential for a process called *methylation.*

Methylation takes place in every cell of your body and ultimately helps you to make important proteins, repair cells, use antioxidants, combat inflammation and support the inflammatory response, eliminate toxins and heavy metals, process fats in the liver, optimize brain function, and silence the genes in your body whose overexpression could cause harm.[1] Variants in the MTHFR gene are common, some of which can fuel headaches, and serious defects are highly correlated with psychiatric symptoms. Methylation also activates the tumor suppressor gene. Therefore, when methylation is under-functioning, the risk for cancer increases.

Roughly half of the population carries mutations in this gene—and the more gene mutations you have, the less effectively the MTHFR enzyme can do its job. You don't, however, have to run out and test your genes to see if you have a defective MTHFR gene. The recommendations I'll be making in the program will support your body's healthy methylation status.

POTENTIAL TRIGGERS OF TEMPLE HEAD PAIN

You might be surprised to learn that imbalances in reproductive hormones are not always genetically driven. Far from it. Four chief villains are usually causing the chaos:

1. High blood sugar
2. Poor liver detoxification
3. Damaged or compromised reproductive glands
4. Stress

BLOOD SUGAR, THE MOTHER OF ALL HORMONES

Poor blood sugar control tops the list of triggers of temple head pain, and this is often due to too much refined sugars. In some cases, too much fruit consumption can also be a trigger. Even though the primary sugar found in fruit, *fructose*, does not cause a spike in blood sugar upon consumption, its metabolism in the liver can lead to insulin resistance and other metabolic challenges. The consumption of fructose, even when it's coming from fresh whole fruit, is ideally digested with fat and protein to turn the volume down on the body's response to pure fructose. Fun fact: Corn isn't a grain but a fruit, and I've seen patients whose corn consumption causes ovarian cysts, which then leads to abnormal hormone regulation. Eliminate the corn, eliminate the hormone imbalances and headaches.

> *Warning for perimenopausal and menopausal women: Consuming an excess of two fruit servings a day is a very common cause of those illustrious hot flashes and night sweats.*

In females, blood sugar rising too far can lead to estrogen dominance. This can lead to pain in both temples, painful menses, moodiness, and even a bigger butt. When men eat too much sugar, it can cause testosterone to convert to estrogen. This can lead to crying at "chick flicks," loss of motivation, and even man boobs. When you see a man with unusually enlarged breasts, that's likely due to too much estrogen in the system.

> *Man boobs? Sugar will raise testosterone in women but do the opposite in men—lowering testosterone and actually raising estrogen, which then promotes the enlargement of male breast tissue.*

HEALTHY LIVER = HEALTHY HORMONES

The second most common cause of pain in the temples is poor liver detoxification. Hormones, especially estrogen, need to be broken down in the liver after they have served their purpose. One of the liver's main jobs is to control detoxification processes, one of which is called methylation. When the methylation cycle is under-functioning, often from a mutated MTHFR gene or toxins, then hormones can become dysregulated. Unfortunately, the typical approach by many doctors is to add hormones in a bid to "balance" the symptoms of hormone dysregulation. But you can see how this can then put further stress on the liver, which may set the stage for several types of cancer.

The liver is ground zero for the body's overall detoxification, so if it's not working properly, hormonal imbalances are practically inevitable. You may have heard of *non-alcoholic fatty liver disease*, a dangerous condition in which the liver accumulates excessive fat in its cells due to damage. Such damage, which can lead to liver disease, could be caused by chronic alcohol abuse, but in the case of "non-alcoholic" fatty liver, the condition is brought on by other toxins—notably too much sugar or exposure to synthetic chemicals from industrial solvents, pesticides, plastics, and plasticizers such as phthalates. In fact, there's an entire class of compounds called endocrine disrupting chemicals, or EDCs, that are infamous for adversely tinkering with the body's hormonal system.[2]

HAPPY OVARIES = HAPPY HORMONES

The third most common cause of pain in the temples is damaged or poorly functioning reproductive glands. In my experience, such damage can be caused by opportunistic viruses that take advantage of a weak gland or organ and "move in" to further stir trouble. If you're deficient in zinc or thiamine, a herpes virus can proliferate. Physically, when an ovary or testicle is poorly functioning, there typically will be a weakness in the gluteus medius muscle, and there will often be pain accompanying the weakness. This muscle is in the upper buttock area. There is a common acupuncture point for hormones located on the outside of the elbow. When you apply firm pressure, there will be tenderness on the elbow opposite to the side of weakness in patients with hormonal imbalances. A woman whose left ovary is not performing well can manifest a weak and tender right elbow and temple headaches. It may be helpful to firmly rub the outside of the elbow where it is tender.

Hormones are a fine dance for males and especially females. For males, hormone imbalances show up as weight gain and reduced libido, whereas females tend to have more pronounced symptoms due to the more dramatic shifts they experience in hormone levels both within a menstrual cycle and throughout their lives. I should point out that women who take hormones in the form of oral contraceptives or hormone replacement therapy may want to revisit these medicines with their doctor if headaches continue to be a problem. For those who need to take hormones for whatever reason yet suffer from headaches as a result, there may be alternatives (e.g., lower doses, skin patches) that allow you to continue benefiting from the hormones without the side effects. Another solution is to take certain herbs (like milk thistle or thiamine) to help the liver detoxify the hormones (see HeadacheAdvantage.com for my personal recommendations).

Sara suffered from daily temporal headaches. Her dad stated that mosquitoes loved her.

Mosquitoes are attracted to people who are deficient in thiamine (vitamin B1). When there is a thiamine deficiency, the body does not metabolize aldehydes properly. Aldehydes tend to have a fruity aroma to them. If you cannot break these compounds down, you can smell "fruity" to the mosquito, as was the case for Sara. Her thiamine deficiency also left her thyroid and heart under-functioning. A thiamine deficiency can cause estrogen excess—and temporal headaches. We started Sara on a thiamine-rich B-vitamin supplement, and her headaches completely resolved. The mosquitoes were no longer attracted to her. So I ask: Could a simple thiamine supplement be the solution to your temple headaches, elbow pain, energy, mood, mosquito bites, and even heart function?

Finally, I must mention the effects stress can have on hormone balance. Too much toxic stress can change levels of many hormones in the body and go so far as to precipitate endocrine disorders and affect virtually all of the body's processes—including those that are supposed to help you cope with and manage stress. We all have to deal with stress in our lives, but how we go about doing that determines whether we veer our bodies toward vibrant headache-free health or torpedo our chances for success.

CHAPTER 10

PAIN THAT SURROUNDS THE HEAD ("HEADBAND PAIN")

Problem in the Large Intestine

Back in the days of my youth, when I was bodybuilding, pounding whole-head pain was the bane of my existence. As I described in the introduction, a simple adjustment to my upper neck and lower back—the areas associated with the colon through the meridians—healed me almost instantly, and it changed the trajectory of my life.

Common Symptoms, Signs, and/or Characteristics Associated with "Headband" Pain

☐ *Headaches that feel like a tight headband*
☐ *Pain in the flank of the lower back*
☐ *Pain in the thumb*
☐ *Pain on the outside of the thighs (IT band syndrome)*
☐ *Abdominal pain*
☐ *Abdominal weight gain*

- ☐ Sensitivity to dairy
- ☐ Frequent sickness
- ☐ Sinus congestion
- ☐ Chronic cough
- ☐ Less than one bowel movement per day on average
- ☐ Sensitivity to corn
- ☐ Lingering cough after a cold
- ☐ Poor sleep between 5 and 7 AM
- ☐ Benefit from probiotics
- ☐ Urinary tract infections
- ☐ Prostatitis (inflamed prostate)
- ☐ Yeast infections
- ☐ Acne, especially in the forehead area
- ☐ Erratic heartbeats
- ☐ Carbohydrate cravings
- ☐ Obstinacy
- ☐ Poor sleep
- ☐ Grief
- ☐ Sadness
- ☐ Yearning
- ☐ Stinky bowel movements

According to a 2023 study, lower back pain is the leading cause of disability around the world, with an estimated 75 to 85 percent of Americans experiencing some form of back pain during their life.[1] When you search online for common causes of lower back pain, the top contenders are the usual suspects: sprains, strains, injuries, fractures, herniated discs, sciatica, osteoarthritis, and spinal stenosis.

But what about digestive problems in the large intestine? There is an extreme miss in the literature to recognize the power of a weak colon in triggering back pain. In addition to lower back pain signaling a colon imbalance, other symptoms include IT band pain, sinus pressure, thumb pain, rheumatoid arthritis, neck pain, and even a cough.

> *Uncommon signs of imbalances in the colon: lower back pain, IT band pain, sinus pressure, thumb pain, rheumatoid arthritis, neck pain, a persistent cough, and a brownish ring around the pupil.*

The muscles that get very tight when the colon is compromised are the *quadratus lumborum* muscles, which are the deepest back muscles. This is the cause of flank-area lower back pain. Also, the muscles on the outside of the thigh may become weak and tender when there is a colon problem. Vertebrae that get tender might include the bones near the top of the neck, the second cervical, and the second and fourth lumbar vertebrae. The second cervical adjustment was the one that changed my life and eliminated my whole-head headaches.

The late Dr. Bernard Jensen, founder of iridology, which examines the eyes for clues to health conditions, identified brown coloring around the pupil to be a sign of colon congestion. This may be another easy identifier for you to decide how relevant colon health is for you.

Yeast overgrowth in the colon can also be part of this picture. Overgrowth can manifest as one-sided neck pain, brain fog, pain at the sacroiliac joint, pain in the front of the shoulder, carb cravings, a coated tongue, kneecap-area pain, pain around the first lumbar vertebra, lower abdominal pain, and/or dry skin (especially on the feet).

I have found yeast overgrowth to cause a weakness in the little iliacus muscle that passes from the pelvis through the groin on either side of the body. This is likely due to the chronic opening of certain valves in the area (namely the ileocecal valve or a so-called Houston's valve). These valves open to protectively move the yeast-feeding undigested carbohydrates out of the intestine before they can further ferment. Referred pain when these valves are open is over the bicep tendon in the front of the shoulder. There will often also be pain in the lower abdomen on either the right or left side over the affected valve. It is the iliacus's weakness that then triggers pain and weakness of the muscles at the back of the neck and the sacroiliac joint.

The most common cause of yeast overgrowth? You should know the answer by now: overconsumption of refined sugar. Yeast overgrowth perpetuates carbohydrate cravings, and on goes the cycle of sugar-yeast-cravings-sugar and the proliferation of bad bacteria. Sugar consumption, in fact, temporarily shuts down the immune system (namely the activity of white blood cells) for approximately four hours upon eating it. Many people don't make it four hours before consuming their next sugary food, so the immune system is never really functioning properly. When yeast and bad bacteria rapidly multiply, a person could develop a leaky gut, which can lead to brain fog and arthritis, as well as more sugar cravings that go on to fuel a vicious cycle of poor blood sugar control. A good indication of blood sugar instability is the number of times one wakes up at night. People often try to blame drinking water late in the evening, but the reality is that when blood sugar dips, it is registered as a crisis in the brain. So, the brain sends out alerting signals that result in midnight awakenings.

> *Midnight awakenings: How many times do you wake up at night? The alarm could very well be your brain telling you that your blood sugar is too low, which itself is indicative of blood sugar imbalances.*

When blood sugar goes up and down, it causes estrogen dominance that can lead to pain on the outside of the elbow (lateral epicondylitis). The ongoing blood sugar imbalances promote weight gain and fat retention. One of the more extreme examples of chronic blood sugar problems is poor circulation. When this circulatory problem is unmanaged, which is often the case in people with long-term type 2 diabetes, the medical intervention might require the removal of dead toes or limbs.

POTENTIAL TRIGGERS OF TEMPLE HEAD PAIN

Linda had been under my care for nearly two years when she finally mentioned whole-head headaches, right outer thigh pain, and chronic diarrhea. Fortunately, a few questions allowed me to easily determine that all these symptoms were a direct result of the milk she had been regularly consuming. She too grew up hearing that milk "does a body good." In her case as an O blood type, however, the milk was feeding yeast, leading to chronic diarrhea. It was adversely affecting the colon, which led to whole-head pain and pain/weakness in the right outer thigh (iliotibial (IT) band). This IT band gets weak and tender when the colon on the same side of the body is functioning abnormally. There is a condition called *IT band syndrome* that often affects running or cycling athletes and which manifests from abnormal colon function. After switching her daily glass of milk to non-dairy alternatives like almond, oat, rice, and macadamia "milks," she no longer suffered from headaches, diarrhea, or pain on the outside of her right thigh.

> *As we discussed about wheat's duplicitous behavior, milk protein is identical to the protein structure of the pancreas. This is another unfortunate example of molecular mimicry in which the immune system attacks the pancreas due to the presence of the milk protein that breaches the leaky gut barrier and enters the bloodstream.*

There are some common lifestyle choices that could cause colon problems and, in turn, whole-head pain, back pain, thumb pain, leg pain, poor sleep, a weakened immune system, or even arthritic aches. Honorable mentions for colon problems include the following:

1. Exposure to glyphosate (typically from wheat or corn)
2. Lack of organic vegetables in the diet
3. Beef (for A blood types)
4. Dehydration
5. Dairy
6. Sugar consumption
7. Parasites

As I've already covered, glyphosate has been shown to not only damage the intestinal lining but also reduce bile production. A damaged intestinal lining can lead to conditions like colitis, in which whole-head pain may be an early warning sign. When bile production is reduced, fats don't get broken down properly. Then, the valves in the intestine (ileocecal and valve of Houston) close to afford the body more time to assimilate the needed good fats.

Organic vegetables are shown to have thousands of times the amount of minerals in them, as well as being pesticide-free. My favorite statement when justifying the expense to patients is that *"organic is cheaper than chemo."* Pesticides and the toxic metals in them are a common cause of cancer. Additionally, the minerals in organic vegetables help rebuild and maintain the tight junctions of the intestinal lining—thus reducing inflammation and challenges to the immune system. The chlorophyll in green leafy vegetables is healing for the intestinal lining and is a precursor for hormones. Of course, the fiber in the vegetables also keeps the food moving properly through the colon and cleanses the intricate brush border of the colon.

It helps to know that if you're type A or AB, consuming beef can be problematic (but for type O, beef is one of the most beneficial foods). When people with blood type A or AB consume beef or most red meats, it can cause colon spasms. When the colon spasms, then the muscles in the lower back flank area spasm. Fish and poultry will not have this effect on you A's and ABs. Next time you "inadvertently" consume red meat and pork, watch for whole-head pain, back spasms, and/or low energy to follow.

> *What's the beef? If you're an A or AB blood type, eating red meat could be causing colon spasms that you feel as lower back pain and that also refer to the whole head. The next time you have a whole-head headache, ask yourself: Did you eat red meat recently?*

One of the key roles of the colon is to remove water from fecal material. If you're dehydrated, then there is less water to remove, and the material becomes denser and more sluggish. A simple fix is to be more diligent about getting in at least eight glasses per day of clean, properly filtered water. The general rule of thumb for volume of water is half your weight in ounces. For example, a 150-pound person should try to consume 75 ounces of clean, filtered water per day.

Approximately 82 percent of the population are either A or O blood types. For both blood types, dairy causes a lot of mucus secondary to its adverse effects on the colon. This can lead to a weakening of the immune system, sinus congestion, neck tension, lower back pain, and/or whole-head pain. The dairy protein simply does not digest well for most people. Pasteurized milk seems to be the most offensive of dairy options. I find that most A or O blood types can tolerate quality yogurt up to two times per week. Mozzarella, goat, and feta cheeses also seem to be better-tolerated cheeses, whereas cheddar and American are more prone to cause symptoms of mucus and immune weakness.

Parasites, including worms, are another common cause of colon imbalances. They often hang out in the last part of the colon, which is part of why an itchy bottom is considered a hallmark symptom of parasites. In addition to the symptoms of colon dysfunction already mentioned, symptoms of parasites flourishing include an itchy bottom, poor sleep, anxiety, seizures, tremors, rashes, and/or skin tags. The brain's primary inhibitory chemical is called GABA (gamma-aminobutyric acid). GABA tends to become low when the body is fighting parasites. The GABA deficiency can then lead to poor sleep quality, anxiety, tremors, or, in children, obstinate behavior.

> *Signs of parasites that could be mucking up your colon:*
> *itchy anus, poor sleep, anxiety, seizures, tremors, rashes,*
> *and / or skin tags.*

Although we like to think we live in a clean first-world environment free from parasites, they are still around and can make their way into our systems. Pets, sushi, and lettuce, especially when combined with low stomach acid, are some of the primary sources of parasites. One year, my wife and I went on a bike trip in Mexico with three other couples. We all ate and drank the same thing. But my wife and I took a supplement that triggered a boost of stomach acid. We were the only ones who did not get laid up for two weeks with Montezuma's revenge.

THE SINUS CONUNDRUM SOLVED

Almost everyone has experienced the pain and pressure of a sinus headache during a cold or flu, accompanied by nasal congestion (stuffy nose). But contrary to popular wisdom, most sinus headaches are not caused by a sinus infection (sinusitis), and they may not be related to an invading germ.

Most sinus problems are caused by any of the same issues we've already covered—primary triggers in the stomach, gallbladder, colon, immune system, thyroid, or an allergy. This means you can identify the culprit by noting where your sinus pain is emanating from. If the sinus problem is left-sided, it's the stomach; if it's right-sided, the gallbladder needs attention. If the sinus congestion is coming from both sides ("whole head") with thick, possibly green mucus flowing out of the nose and bowel movements that are fewer than one per day, it's a colon problem.

If the sinus problem involves clear and/or watery mucus, it could be either an allergy or a thyroid condition. In the case of an allergic reaction, there will likely be sneezing or watery eyes associated with it. One would likely do well to correct a weakness in the lungs or stomach. Look for triggers in your environment such as mold, dust, or noxious chemicals from products.

CAN YOU KEEP THE COFFEE?

A Cautionary Note about Coffee: A very common cause of chronic sinus congestion is coffee consumption.

- This consequence is exaggerated if you are adding a dairy product to your coffee (creamer, anyone?). Both dairy and coffee can disrupt the digestive process and trigger sinus congestion. I won't suggest that everyone avoid coffee entirely, but you should limit consumption to two or fewer cups a day and consider switching your caffeine source to green tea.

Green tea contains caffeine, but it also includes the amino acid threonine, which helps to reduce the negative side effects of caffeine. It also contains other good compounds that act as potent antioxidants with protective effects on blood sugar balance, cardiovascular health, fat metabolism, and even cognition.

PART III

ENDING YOUR PAIN WITH THE H.E.A.D. PROGRAM

CHAPTER 11

HEAL THE MAIN TRIGGER/ WEAKNESS

Solutions to the Common Culprits

Twenty years before Kathleen had her first appointment with me, she'd sustained a skull fracture. Seven years prior to our meeting, a surgical mesh was implanted in an attempt to relieve what was diagnosed as trigeminal neuralgia—a type of facial chronic pain that's so severe and debilitating that it can lead some to contemplate suicide. The excruciating pain feels like a jabbing electric shock on one side of the face, and the sensation moves from the face to the brain. The attacks can last seconds to minutes and come in waves that go on for days or longer.

For Kathleen, this was a reasonable diagnosis considering she had daily left-sided head pain that followed the trigeminal nerve. She was also experiencing vision loss in her left eye and had been told that frequent use of steroid eye drops could have been causing that. The steroid drops were an attempt to reduce head pain. Kathleen also complained of an "upset stomach," pain in her right buttock (piriformis muscle), and frequent urination. Her primary reason for seeing me was the pain in her right buttock, as she had mentally resigned to the fact that she would have head pain for the rest of her life.

In craniosacral therapy, a hands-on massage technique that gently releases tension in the skull and spine, it's well known that poor movement of the parietal bones of the skull, the spot where Kathleen had suffered the fracture and where the mesh had been implanted, can cause poor stomach functioning. After my examination, I "prescribed" a regimen of supplements that would help heal her stomach. Due to my schedule, we were unable to follow up with her until six weeks later, at which point most of her head pain had vanished and she no longer complained of stomach discomfort. She had just seen another chiropractor for lower back pain in the flank area, an indication her colon was functioning poorly. At that visit, we tripled her stomach supplement dosage, and Kathleen finally had her turnaround. She's feeling fantastic, with no more trigeminal neuralgia or lower back pain.

Kathleen's story may sound too good to be true, but I've got hundreds if not thousands of others just like hers. May you be one of them!

You've come a long way by this point in the book in terms of learning about the seven different pain patterns of headaches, and you've probably picked up on several potential solutions. I've saved the bulk of my recommendations for this part of the book, where you'll gain more in-depth knowledge and a step-by-step plan of action using the H.E.A.D. protocol:

⇒ **H**: Heal the main weakness
⇒ **E**: Edit your diet and environment
⇒ **A**: Allow for sleep, exercise, and stress reduction
⇒ **D**: Dedicate

In this chapter, we start with the H part of the program, which gives ideas specific to your type of headache. I'm going to cover the basics to address the seven pain sources. I'll go through each type of headache, starting with a flowchart that presents typical symptoms of a particular headache and the top solutions to treat them. In most cases, the solutions here entail a combination of supplements or other ingredients to address certain organs, tissues, and glands. Reducing or avoiding certain ingredients will also be recommended in some instances. Broader recommendations offered in the next chapters will help round out your overall protocol.

Although you may think that only one type of headache affects you, it's common to alleviate one type and then encounter another due to an additional hidden weakness in the body. As happens with many of my patients, healing the body can mean addressing more than one organ, tissue, or system. Be patient and methodical in this process. Everybody is unique, and you may need to try different things to test various solutions. These flowcharts are designed to help you map your symptoms to specific solutions, but they are not *rigid*—you may find yourself identifying several symptoms across the spectrum, for which a combination of remedies is in order.

> *Use the flowcharts to make sense of your symptoms and begin to find solutions. This is not a black-and-white endeavor, however. These charts were constructed in a way that most people would be able to relate to a single column, but you may find yourself relating to several symptoms across the spectrum. Don't hesitate to try a combination of potential solutions.*

For example, if you suffer from left-sided headaches due to low stomach acid, you might see in the first flowchart that you can relate to many of the symptoms across all four categories, for which a combination therapy of supplements is helpful. However, you will likely find yourself mostly aligned with a vertical pattern of symptoms, and I would suggest that you start with that solution. In this example, start with ginger or an HCl product (brand recommendations of which can be found at HeadacheAdvantage. com). Unless specifically noted below, you'll find dosage recommendations where appropriate at HeadacheAdvantage.com.

If, after implementing the primary potential solution, you still have challenges, consider the next vertical progression that relates to you. Most of my patients find they can identify with one cluster of symptoms down one of the "columns." It will probably be helpful to refer back to the checklists in Part II and note which boxes you marked as your prime symptoms.

LEFT-SIDED HEADACHES: TREAT THE STOMACH

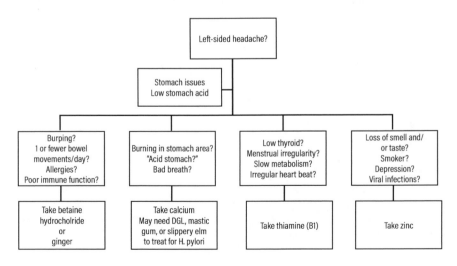

For more information and to order these fine supplements, go to www.HeadacheAdvantage.com.

As you'll recall, when pain is located on the left side of the head, it is often caused by low stomach acid. Proper stomach acid production is an energy-intensive process that requires many inputs, including adequate water, zinc, B1, and calcium. A deficiency of any one of these ingredients can lead to poor stomach function. The four columns above reflect the four main buckets of triggers for low stomach acid. For many who can identify with column 1, taking hydrochloric acid in supplement form can be enormously helpful. The spice ginger is also shown to help stimulate stomach acid production, and you can find ginger in many forms.

> *When stomach function is compromised or you have gut dysbiosis due to an imbalance of microbiota, you're more vulnerable to developing an autoimmune condition.*[1]

People with "acid stomach" (column 2) wrongly think they need to take antacids when all they really need is calcium. Antacid medications and over-the-counter acid-blocking medications block the proper functioning of the stomach. This blocking of stomach function can refer pain to the left side of the head. Even worse, blocking the proper functioning of the stomach can create an environment where autoimmune conditions can develop. Antacids can also lead to bone loss by inhibiting the absorption of calcium.

The tricky thing about calcium is that we need calcium to make and buffer stomach acid, but we also need stomach acid to liberate calcium. See the rut we can get stuck in? The form of most supplements is critical, which is why I have dedicated a page on my website to sharing brand ideas and particular ingredients to look out for. Because the supplement industry is woefully unregulated, you need to be sure you're acquiring the best of the best. In the calcium department, for instance, I find calcium lactate (260 mg Ca/ 50 mg), as opposed to calcium carbonate, to be ideal for helping break this vicious cycle. Deglycyrrhizinated licorice (DGL), mastic gum, and, for those with too much *H. pylori*, slippery elm can also be helpful. You may not know if you have too much *H. pylori* unless you've already been diagnosed with a related condition, such as gastritis or a peptic ulcer. But even without knowing, if you have an ache or burning sensation in your stomach, especially pain that's worse when your stomach is empty, you would do well to try a combo of calcium, DGL, mastic gum, and slippery elm (possibly found in a single supplement) to see if that helps you find relief from both the burn and the headaches.

Correcting for thyroid dysfunction (column 3), which you now know can contribute to left-sided headaches as well as tension-type headaches, is relatively easy to fix with proper supplementation. Many foods, especially grains in the U.S., are "fortified" with vitamin B1 in a form that requires energy to become useful for optimum human function. A more ideal form of B1 would be a phosphorylated version known as cocarboxylase chloride or the form that comes from foods like liver. We use thiamine to make energy from carbohydrate metabolism, to aid in thyroid function, and to help the formation of stomach acid.

Zinc deficiencies can be caused by a variety of issues, from not obtaining enough from the diet or poorly absorbing it to invading viruses and toxic exposures to metals, which can happen with tobacco use.

Zinc deficiency (column 4) can trigger many symptoms. Viruses and/or exposure to toxic metals through smoking and even old tattoos are frequently the main culprits of a zinc deficiency. This is why so many people lost their sense of smell and taste after their immune system used up the zinc stores in fighting the COVID virus. It is also why people who have smoked for years tend to gain weight after they stop smoking. The toxic metals like cadmium and arsenic being inhaled cause a zinc deficiency. Then when they stop, food tastes good again.

Interestingly, adding zinc to a smoking cessation program can be tremendously helpful, as it often makes cigarettes less enjoyable. Zinc also helps metabolize the stress hormone cortisone, which may inhibit stomach acid production. Bonus: Zinc has hormone-balancing properties and facilitates proper immune system function.

Although a zinc deficiency has long been associated with feelings of depression and anxiety, not until 2017 did researchers at NYU link zinc to those famous neurotransmitters—dopamine and serotonin—that double as hormones and play into our neural processes and emotions.[2] Another study, this one done in 2021, found that one of the ways zinc elevates these important neurotransmitters is through its positive effects on boosting levels of a critical growth factor called brain-derived neurotrophic factor (BDNF) *in the areas of the brain that control emotions.*[3] No surprise then that when zinc levels fall, BDNF levels fall too, and our mood takes a dip.

In addition to taking zinc in supplement form, seeded vegetables, especially pumpkin seeds, are a great source of zinc.

Nutritional sources of zinc: pumpkin seeds, chickpeas, lentils, hemp seeds, eggs, meat, oysters, crab, and meat.

RIGHT-SIDED HEADACHES: TREAT THE GALLBLADDER

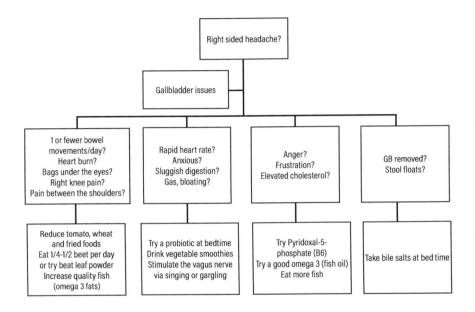

For more information and to order these fine supplements, go to www.HeadacheAdvantage.com.

As a reminder, gallbladder-related symptoms often strike on the right side of the body. Symptoms include right sinus congestion, right knee or ankle weakness, right upper abdominal pain, heartburn, constipation, poor recall, elevated blood pressure and cholesterol, and, of course, right-sided headaches. No matter which column you identify with here, you'd do well to consider all of the following top strategies to fix a broken gallbladder:

More beets and beet greens: These superfood vegetables are well documented to boost gallbladder function, notably by enhancing bile production and thinning the bile so it flows more easily, in addition to providing vitamins, minerals, antioxidants, fiber, and other health-promoting plant compounds.[4] They also may help protect your heart health, reduce high blood pressure, and benefit your digestive system. Beets are incredibly versatile and can be eaten raw or lightly cooked, though raw is optimal to gain the most nutrients. Add grated raw beets to salads or use them for dipping into hummus or guacamole. Beet greens taste similar to kale, and they make for a great side dish when sauteed in olive oil, garlic, and lemon juice. You can also consider a beet-based supplement. Again, see my website for specific recommendations.

Eating more detoxifying vegetables is a good idea to help neutralize bad apples, so to speak, that we inadvertently consume. It's hard to eliminate all the exposures we endure on a daily basis, no matter how "green" we think we are living. The powerhouse veggies in this department that will support your body's internal detoxification system include asparagus, broccoli, Brussels sprouts, artichokes, collard greens, avocado, kale, cauliflower, radishes, spinach, and cabbage. You can blend up a smoothie with some of these gems and toss in some detoxifying fruits too for added sweetness—fruits like blueberries and cherries. Adding a sugar-free Greek yogurt will further give a boost to the super smoothie by contributing a dose of probiotics that will assist with decreasing inflammation, which will automatically help support detoxification and immune health. For those who do not enjoy probiotic-rich foods like yogurt and fermented vegetables, a probiotic taken at bedtime is recommended.

More quality fats: The gallbladder contracts and ejects bile into the small intestine in the presence of fats. When we consume good quality fats, then the gallbladder virtually cleanses itself while aiding in our detoxification and bolstering our immune system. When the liver cleanses toxins from the blood, it sends them to the bile to be ejected into the intestine for elimination when we eat good fat. The key is to avoid fried and greasy foods high in saturated and trans fats in favor of monounsaturated and polyunsaturated fats found in fatty fish, nuts, seeds, avocados, and oils like olive, macadamia, flax seed, walnut, and avocado. Instead of traditional butter, try ghee, which is a saturated fat from clarified butter that also shows benefits for healthy skin and gallbladder function. You can add an omega-3 supplement to your diet (see HeadacheAdvantage.com) if you're not a big fish lover.

> *Consuming high-quality fats will detox and cleanse the gallbladder and fortify your immune system.*

For people with high cholesterol, a dietary fat deficiency could be why the body overcompensates by manufacturing more cholesterol. Quality fats, including the right balance of cholesterol, are key to producing hormones—many of which are essential for mood, memory, and regulating your heart and blood pressure—and any deficit in those ingredients will have adverse effects. If you're someone who identifies a lot with column 3 in the flowchart, adding a B6 supplement is also recommended (see page xx for more about B6, and go to my website to find brand ideas for choosing the most active form).

Fewer pesticides: While all of us should avoid exposure to pesticides/herbicides, those with gallbladder and stomach problems should be especially vigilant. As discussed, glyphosate can inhibit bile production as well as damage intestinal cells. Wherever possible, choose organic foods, particularly when buying produce, corn and soy products, and oats and whole wheat products, including Ezekiel breads.

Eliminate tomatoes: For those with blood type A or B, I find tomato-based products to drastically inhibit the proper functioning of the gallbladder. Yes, that includes ketchup and salsa, unfortunately. Eating tomato products is a common cause of heartburn, which may lead to elevated blood pressure, recall problems, abdominal pains, and/or elevated cholesterol. Even if you don't know your blood type (see page xx), try to nix tomatoes and tomato-based products from your diet.

Added Tip: Recall that the brain controls the gallbladder via a chemical called acetylcholine. If your symptoms are dominated by memory challenges and elevated blood pressure along with more typical gallbladder symptoms (right-sided headaches, right knee pain, right eye symptoms, or constipation and abdominal pain), then you may do well with more of the nutrient choline. Choline is found in many foods, chiefly eggs, cruciferous vegetables (such as broccoli and Brussels sprouts), and some types of nuts, beans, and seeds. Often, it's hard to get enough through food alone, so a supplement can help (see website for brand recommendations).

For those without a gallbladder: Anyone who has had their gallbladder already removed for whatever reason knows the drill, especially right after the surgery. You can live a normal life without a gallbladder by avoiding high-fat fried foods and eating more fiber, as your liver should make enough bile to digest your food. The bile the liver makes will drop into your digestive system rather than being stored in a gallbladder. But the loss of the gallbladder does mean you could end up with a bile deficiency, for which bile salts in supplement form are helpful. Pale-colored, floating stools and bad-smelling gas are typical signs of a bile salt deficiency. If you do choose a bile salt supplement, it's important to stay up on your hydration. About 85 percent of bile is water, so you don't want to be dehydrated.

BACK-HEAD ("TENSION") HEADACHES

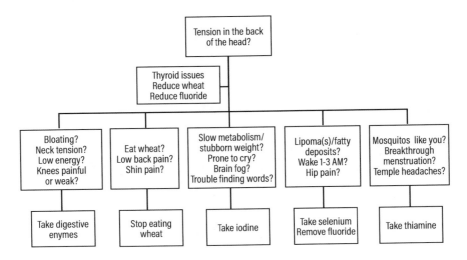

For more information and to order these fine supplements, go to www.HeadacheAdvantage.com.

As described in Chapter 6, thyroid issues dominate in people who suffer from back-head ("tension-type") headaches. Thyroid conditions are extraordinarily common, especially among women—one in eight will experience thyroid problems in her lifetime. It's no wonder that thyroid medication is among the most prescribed drugs, even more so than cholesterol-lowering medications. The thyroid is a master gland that receives feedback from many other glands, which makes it very vulnerable to imbalances. The thyroid can easily become imbalanced from toxic exposures (e.g., metals, fluoride), blood sugar chaos, deficiencies in iodine or thiamine, poor stress tolerance, and estrogen imbalances.

If you find yourself following one of the columns above in the flowchart to match your specific symptoms, you can target which solution earns top priority. You can also take a broad approach and try a combination of potential remedies:

Try digestive enzymes: A sluggish thyroid can have an impact on the gastrointestinal system, slowing down your bowel movements and reducing important enzymes needed for proper digestion while preventing the absorption of nutrients. Moreover, the thyroid targets enzymes like *amylase* and *trypsinogen* stored in your digestive system, but it needs to have enough stomach acid on hand to break down carbs, fats, and proteins. If the thyroid is not producing sufficient active T3 hormone (thyroglobulin) to support the right balance of stomach acidity, digestion suffers. This is when taking digestive enzymes is helpful.

Remove thyroid-busting toxins: The top three exposures to reduce or eliminate are wheat, mercury-rich foods (e.g., swordfish, bigeye tuna, and king mackerel), and fluoride. Whole wheat's amino acid sequence is similar to that found in the thyroid, and such "molecular mimicry" can confuse the body and trigger it to attack its own. Wheat can also be tainted with the herbicide glyphosate and have an adverse effect on thyroid cells, reducing their viability and healthy proliferation. Pesticides and herbicides act as thyroid disruptors, with wide-ranging hormone-disrupting effects in the body. Glyphosate in particular is well documented in the literature for raising the risk of thyroid disorders and thyroid cancer. Mercury can similarly harm the thyroid's functionality by binding to cells in the gland and causing hypothyroidism. The heavy metal also can interfere with many of the minerals, such as zinc, magnesium, and selenium, that are necessary for the gland to produce thyroid hormone, as well as to convert T4 to the active T3 form. A lot of people with thyroid and autoimmune thyroid conditions are found to have high levels of mercury in their tissues. Although mercury is found in numerous places—from cosmetics to vaccines—most people are exposed to harmful amounts through fish and dental fillings. What's more, mercury competes with iodine in the thyroid, as they are chemically very similar to each other. The thyroid is an iodine-hungry gland. Approximately 80 percent of the dietary intake of iodine is used by the thyroid, with your mitochondria also using a large amount for energy production.

> *The thyroid is an iodine-hungry gland. Without enough iodine, it will falter.*

Your thyroid is good at absorbing iodine in your body, but when mercury is around, the thyroid will store that in place of iodine. Iodine is the primary building block of these thyroid hormones. T4 (thyroxin) is a tyrosine amino acid with four iodine molecules bound to it. If there is insufficient iodine or tyrosine in the diet, the thyroid can underperform. Incidentally, if there is an autoimmune attack against the thyroid, as in Hashimoto's disease, the wrong form of iodine or some thyroid medications can exaggerate this attack.

About 30 percent of the people in the world are at risk for iodine deficiency.[5] The body doesn't make it, so you absorb the mineral from foods like saltwater fish, shellfish, dairy, and eggs. There's a reason they put iodine in table salt. When people started using iodized salt, iodine deficiency became much less common. But iodized salt is not typically a valuable source of iodine, and if you're deficient due to mercury toxicity or some other reason, supplementing with iodine is helpful.

Fluoride is ubiquitous in public drinking water. It was added to water supplies starting in the 1950s to minimize tooth decay. But when you get too much of it, it can suppress your thyroid. Before the development of thyroid-suppressing medications, fluoride was used to treat an overactive thyroid (hyperthyroidism). You can effortlessly reduce your fluoride ingestion just by using water filters that sift this mineral out.

Supplement where appropriate: An iodine deficiency can fuel a slow thyroid, rendering it unable to manufacture sufficient levels of the critical thyroid hormone. But too much iodine can also backfire on you and have a negative effect on the thyroid. Historically, a fatty deposit called a lipoma developed on my left triceps. Lipomas are benign (noncancerous) growths that propagate slowly under the skin and above the muscle and are commonly found on the neck, shoulders, abdomen, arms, thighs, and back.

For some patients, it's necessary to take a selenium supplement to assist in metabolizing the excess iodine out of the system. Selenium is a mineral key to thyroid function and hormone metabolism; without enough of it, you can develop an overactive thyroid (hyperthyroidism).

TIP: Iodide as a salt or potassium iodide are the forms I find to be less likely to stimulate an autoimmune attack on the thyroid. If you take an iodine supplement and you experience pain in the center of your lower back or feel a racing of your heart, the iodine supplement is likely not well tolerated by your thyroid.

As I've also already covered, thiamine deficiencies fuel a lot of thyroid dysfunction because it's critical for a wide array of reactions in the body. Low levels of thiamine can be a root cause of thyroid issues, and often the thiamine deficiency can be blamed on too much processed carbohydrates. So, in addition to managing your carb intake and keeping blood sugar in check, a thiamine supplement (vitamin B1) can also be helpful.

FRONTAL (FOREHEAD) HEADACHES

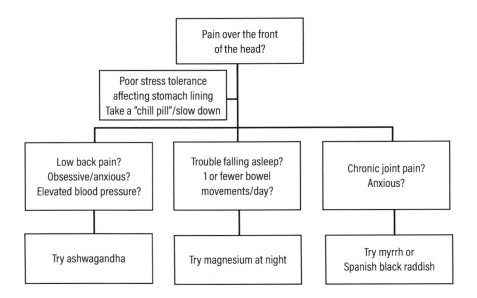

For more information and to order these fine supplements, go to www.HeadacheAdvantage.com.

Chronic, unrelenting stress is the chief villain in frontal headaches. Stress ultimately inflicts damage to the stomach's mucosal lining through its downstream effects on important biochemicals and the balance of key substances that protect that lining. As we discussed in Chapter 7, when the protective barrier of the stomach is compromised, then the body may refer pain to the front of the head, causing frontal headaches. This barrier protects the stomach lining from the very acidic (pH of 2) stomach acid. Potential long-term consequences of a compromised mucus/bicarbonate barrier are ulcers or possibly even stomach cancer.

The key for anyone with frontal headaches is to calm down! I'll be covering a few notable ideas for reducing stress and building habits that fortify your resilience to stress and dampen anxiety. For now, let's review some choice supplements I like that have helped many of my patients chill out and relieve their frontal headaches.

Ashwagandha: One of the most famous adaptogens is this gem of an evergreen shrub that grows in Africa, Asia, and parts of the Middle East. Adaptogens are, by definition, plant substances, including mushrooms, that may help your body to "adapt" to stress and respond better so the stress is less likely to adversely affect you. Ashwagandha in particular has been studied and used for centuries in Ayurvedic medicine for its anti-anxiety, anti-depression, and energy-boosting powers. According to the Cleveland Clinic, ashwagandha "has a positive effect on the endocrine, nervous, immune, and cardiovascular systems by regulating your metabolism and helping you relax by calming how your brain responds to stress. Ashwagandha offers protection for your cells as an antioxidant and reduces swelling (an anti-inflammatory reaction)."[6] Research also shows it can normalize cortisol levels, improve immune function, and even enhance memory. You can find ashwagandha in many forms, from liquid drops and powders to capsules and edibles. A typical dosage is 500 mg twice daily.

Magnesium: Sleep is critical for your entire biology, and when you don't bank quality sleep, you feel it. We've all experienced a bad night's sleep on occasion, but chronic trouble with sleep can become downright dangerous. Magnesium is needed for more than 300 biochemical reactions in the body and is one of the most abundant minerals in the body, serving many roles.[7] In addition to participating in managing blood sugar and pressure, strengthening bones, regulating heart rhythm, and producing energy, it also helps promote sleep through a variety of mechanisms. Three chief ways it helps is through lowering the stress hormone cortisol to counter that fight-or-flight response, regulating certain features of the central nervous system to result in a calming effect, and increasing the release of melatonin.

On studies done to look into magnesium and headaches, some show that migraine sufferers use magnesium to prevent their next headache. The mineral may also help gut motility and lower blood pressure, both of which can further stack the deck in your favor away from that headache. Many foods contain magnesium, such as leafy green vegetables, legumes, nuts, seeds, whole grains, fish, and cultured yogurt. For those who want to try a magnesium supplement before bed, 200–350 mg is a typical dosage for an adult and should be taken 30 minutes before bed.

Myrrh: This oily, sap-like resin from the bark of *Commiphora* trees has been used in ancient Eastern and Egyptian medicine for centuries for its anti-inflammatory, antioxidant, antibacterial, anti-pain, and antiseptic properties. All of these potential benefits ultimately mean myrrh may help improve digestion, boost immunity, and reduce your body's load of stress. In fact, studies show that certain myrrh oil extracts can dramatically reduce headache pain, as well as pain from sore muscles and bad backs.[8] You can find it as an essential oil, gum, or mouthwash.

Spanish black radish: You might not have heard of this root vegetable before, but it's in the same family of cruciferous plants as cabbages, mustard greens, and broccoli. What makes this radish so healing is its high levels of a nutrient called glucosinolate that supports healthy digestion, as well as liver and gallbladder function through its detoxification effects. Typical dosages are up to three a day of a 750 mg tablet (see my site for more).

CYCLOPS HEADACHES

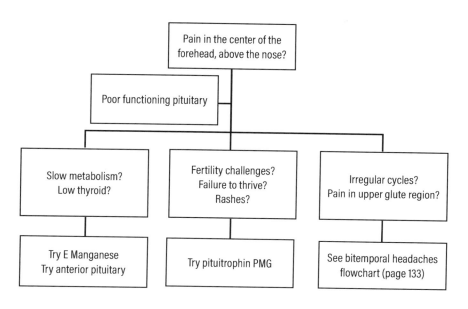

For more information and to order these fine supplements, go to www.HeadacheAdvantage.com.

Cyclops headaches are not as common as the other types, largely because they are caused by an uncommon condition—*a poorly functioning pituitary*. The pituitary is the "air traffic control" HQ for your hormones. So when it's not working properly, your hormonal system will run amok. Its close ties to the hypothalamus and thyroid mean those glands could also be impacted. And even though hormonal imbalances are more common among females, I've treated men whose headaches can be attributed to an underperforming pituitary and who simply need a supplement to support optimal functioning of the gland. Here are some ideas to consider:

Manganese: The trace mineral manganese is found in tiny amounts throughout the body and has wide-ranging effects, as it helps form connective tissue, bones, sex hormones, and blood-clotting factors. It participates in metabolizing fats and carbohydrates, in absorbing calcium, in using vitamins like thiamine, and in regulating blood sugar. As you'll recall, too much sugar consumption can send your hormones off-kilter, and sometimes addressing a sugar addiction is a one-way ticket to fixing a broken pituitary.

Animal studies have shown that a manganese deficiency can impair the action of insulin and disrupt normal blood levels of glucose; moreover, human studies have shown that people with diabetes have lower manganese blood levels, though we don't know if having diabetes causes manganese levels to drop or whether low levels of the mineral contribute to developing diabetes.[9]

Interestingly, it's been estimated that as many as 37 percent of Americans do not get the recommended dietary intake of manganese, which is found in whole grains, leafy vegetables, oysters, clams, mussels, tofu, sweet potatoes, chickpeas, and nuts.[10] Our standard American diet unfortunately processes this important mineral out. In supplement form, manganese is paired with vitamin E to provide extra support to the body's antioxidant system.

Anterior pituitary: This glandular extract, which usually is derived from cows, may help stimulate the pituitary's release of hormones, particularly growth hormone. The anterior pituitary primarily regulates the thyroid by releasing thyroid-stimulating hormone (TSH). It is a less common cause of cyclops headaches but may be relevant in about 20 percent of cases.

Pituitrophin PMG: Another supplement derived from the pituitary glands of cows, Pituitrophin PMG provides nutrients and other ingredients that support the health and function of the pituitary gland.

PAIN IN THE SIDES OF THE HEAD (TEMPLES)

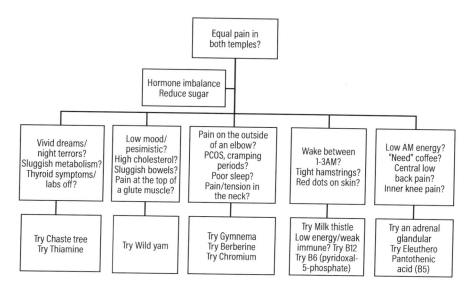

For more details and to order these supplements, go to www. HeadacheAdvantage.com.

Hormonal imbalances encompass a wide territory and can be challenging to address if you don't know exactly where the imbalance is coming from. If your body's chemical messengers are not in harmony with its needs and demands, you will develop symptoms. Those symptoms can be any number of extremely varied and nonspecific signs, from unexplained weight gain or loss to fatigue, muscle weakness, depression, joint pain, dry skin, brittle hair, sensitivity to cold or heat, acne, infertility...the list goes on.

Many hormones naturally fluctuate throughout your days and overall life. Women are especially prone to imbalances given their monthly cycles, but men can have imbalances too. Hormone imbalances can also be associated with other chronic conditions like high blood pressure, high cholesterol, and diabetes. Some imbalances that are linked to serious disorders with certain hormone-producing reproductive glands may need traditional medical therapies, but most imbalances can be addressed naturally through lifestyle changes.

You can do a lot to bring your hormones into balance with a proper diet that's low in sugar and high in quality nutrients. Getting rid of excess weight can also help, as that extra fat is a hormone-producing tissue that can further throw a wrench into your system. People who maintain the ideal weight for them are less likely to have hormonal issues.

> *Dietary changes that reduce sugar and deliver high-quality nutrients can both stimulate weight loss and help balance hormones.*

Use the chart above to see if you identify with any of the columns flowing down. Here are some tidbits about the supplements listed that have not yet been defined (for dosing and brand ideas, see my website):

Chaste tree: This shrub's medicinal parts are the dried fruit and leaves, and they have had a long history in balancing hormones, particularly in treating menstrual cycle problems and pain, as well as menopause. The herb comes in the form of capsules, liquid extracts, and tinctures and may help stimulate progesterone.

Wild yam: Of the more than 600 species of this plant, 12 are edible, but consuming wild yam is not common because of its bitter taste. Wild yam contains a chemical called diosgenin that can influence the body's production of several hormones, most notably estrogen. It also has been shown to regulate blood sugar levels. The supplement has been used for a range of conditions, including menopause symptoms, cramps, muscular pain, blood sugar imbalances, and even rheumatoid arthritis, given its anti-inflammatory properties. You'll find this supplement in a variety of formulations, from tablets and capsules to powders and teas.

Gymnema: A woody vine plant native to India, Africa, and Australia that's been used for centuries in Ayurvedic medicine, gymnema contains compounds that may assist the insulin-signaling system by reducing how much sugar gets absorbed in the stomach, increasing cellular growth in the pancreas, reducing sugar cravings, and boosting the amount of insulin in the body. As such, it's been used for metabolic disorders such as obesity, diabetes, and high cholesterol.

Berberine: This plant-derived chemical shot to fame when weight loss drugs like Ozempic recently took the stage. The chemical has been shown in multiple studies to help regulate sugar and fat metabolism, thus making it a candidate for treating many conditions, from metabolic ones to those that affect the heart. One of berberine's mechanisms is its activation of an important enzyme inside cells called AMP-activated protein kinase (AMPK), which has a starring role in regulating metabolism and energy levels.

Chromium: An essential trace element, chromium forms a compound in the body that can lower blood sugar levels and improve insulin sensitivity. You can get this mineral from soil-grown foods such as vegetables, fruits, and whole grains, but as we've discussed, our mineral-depleted soils can make it harder to obtain all the minerals we need through food alone.

Milk thistle: Most moms with newborns will know this supplement, as it's often recommended to help support the production of breast milk, but it's also long been used to treat several metabolic, liver, and gallbladder conditions. The plant's seeds contain a group of bioflavonoids called silymarin that is known to protect the liver by preventing toxins from attaching to liver cells, lower blood sugar levels, prevent insulin resistance, lower cholesterol, and even slow the growth of cancer.

Vitamin B12 (cobalamin): As we covered in Chapter 9, vitamin B12 is essential for methylation—a complex process throughout the body's cells that ultimately affects how it functions and which genes get expressed. When it comes to hormones, B12 is needed for methylation in the liver alongside B6, folate, and other nutrients to successfully break down excess hormones (such as estrogen) and cellular waste. One of the signs of a B12 deficiency (and hormone imbalance) is high homocysteine levels in the blood and urine. Homocysteine is a toxic, inflammatory amino acid compound that requires B12 for its proper metabolism. Another sign of a deficiency is poor flexibility, as there's a tightening of the fascia around the muscles that makes one feel stiff. When seeking a B12 supplement, look for the methylcobalamin form (as opposed to the cyanocobalamin form—see HeadacheAdvantage. com for my favorite B12 supplement).

Vitamin B6 (pyridoxal-5-phosphate, or P5P): This B vitamin plays a big role in keeping the body's balance of different hormones. It's often used to help women with progesterone deficiencies or who have excessive or reduced levels of testosterone. Vitamin B6 is also needed in the creation of adrenal hormones and is a primary player in the formation or breakdown of about 70 percent of the brain's neurotransmitters.

Adrenal glandular: Your adrenal glands sit on top of your kidneys and make certain hormones like cortisol and adrenaline to help control your body's response to stress. Adrenal extracts are made from the adrenals of other animals, such as cows and pigs, and they are frequently used for a variety of ailments, such as low adrenal function, fatigue, allergies and asthma, poor stress tolerance, hypoglycemia, autoimmune disorders, pain and swelling, and some skin conditions.

Eleuthero: Also called Siberian ginseng, eleuthero comes from a woody shrub but is not a true ginseng. It has been used traditionally as a stimulant and immune system booster and is typically classified as an adaptogen. Among the potential benefits of this fruit-producing plant are increased energy and blood flow, improved memory retention, enhancement of the body's healing mechanisms, and boosted endurance during exercise. In the hormonal department, eleuthero has been shown to lower or stabilize blood sugar levels, reduce insulin resistance, and ease the effects of estrogen withdrawal in menopausal women.

Vitamin B5 (pantothenic acid): Sometimes called the anti-stress vitamin, this water-soluble B vitamin is necessary for the body's synthesis of coenzyme A (CoA), which helps turn food into energy and is essential for the metabolism of fatty acids. It's also needed to make and metabolize our macronutrients (fats, proteins, and carbs), as well as produce hormones and cholesterol. Moreover, it helps break down acetylcholine; if acetylcholine builds up, symptoms may include anxiety and panic attacks. Gut bacteria can produce some of the vitamin B5 we need but not the amount we need, so we must get it from foods or supplements. Headaches are among the top symptoms when you're deficient in this vitamin.

I have listed signs and symptoms that you may need a herb like wild yam, chaste tree, berberine, gymnema, milk thistle, or eleuthero. I have also listed the symptoms associated with B12, B6, B5, or adrenal glandular products. This list is intended as a guide to help you determine which product most resonates with your individual needs. Start with the ONE that most closely matches your pattern. The best, typically physician-only versions of these products can be found at www.HeadacheAdvantage.com.

PAIN THAT SURROUNDS THE HEAD ("HEADBAND PAIN")

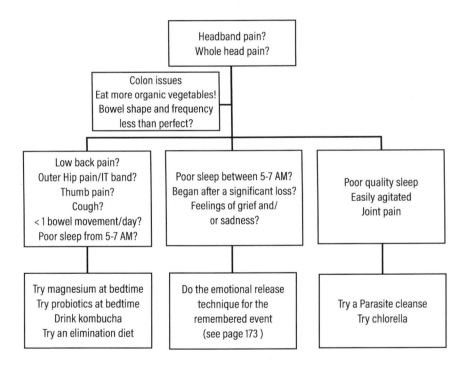

For more information on top-quality products associated with these categories, visit www.HeadacheAdvantage.com.

Headband pain is a colon problem, and colon problems demand a multifaceted approach to solving that involves cleaning up your dietary habits, identifying any offending foods or ingredients in your diet that don't work with your system, and considering some colon-friendly supplements. Colon problems can be caused by glyphosate exposure (wheat and corn), a lack of vegetables, dehydration, and dairy or sugar consumption. These are the most common triggers I see clinically.

In addition to the headband headache, you may also experience other pains with an ill-functioning colon. Muscles in the lower back and outside of the thigh, for example, may become weak and tender. There may be pain in the back of the neck or front of the shoulder. Sinuses may get congested. Your thumb(s) may feel sore, and joint pains may flair. Brain fog may slow you down.

If you have pain in the back of the head, the thyroid is likely the cause of the colon-induced whole-head pain (review the tension headache section on page 134 for more targeted solutions for you). If you also experience left-sided head pain, constipation, allergies, and/or abdominal distress, then you would do well to start with the left-sided headache section. If solutions there don't solve your issues promptly or don't resonate with you, then dig into the following potential strategies. Similarly, if you experience right-sided headaches, pain behind the knee, and/or heartburn in addition to whole-head pain, you would likely do well to first look at the potential solutions in the right-sided headache section before considering the following ideas.

POTENTIAL SOLUTIONS FOR WHOLE-HEAD PATTERN PAIN

Probiotics: Consider probiotics if you have one or fewer satisfying bowel movements per day, have forehead acne, have blood sugar instability, wake up or sleep poorly between 5 and 7 AM, have flank-area lower back pain, and/or tend to get sick more than once per year. The challenge with recommending probiotics in a format like this book is that each species of probiotics can have very different functions. For example, *Saccharomyces* tends to help more if the bowel movements are unformed. *Lactobacillus*-based probiotics may help you produce needed vitamin B12. *Bifidobacterium* may have value in stabilizing blood sugar. Experiment with different types of probiotics that contain multiple species to see which ones work best for you. Probiotic products are usually best taken at bedtime. If you are sick, it may even help to dose high with as many as six capsules at bedtime for the first week or two, before reducing to one to three capsules at bedtime. Think about consuming natural sources of probiotics too, such as fermented vegetables, cultured yogurt, and kombucha tea.

Elimination diet: When something in your diet is causing inflammation in your digestive system, it's essential to figure out what ingredient could be stirring up trouble. Top offenders include dairy, wheat, corn, potatoes, processed/packaged foods, added sugars, and unhealthy fats. Start by eliminating any key food we've already discussed, and keep them out for at least three days to see how much better your overall pain and digestion are. If symptoms do not improve, keep eliminating potential triggers for another three days until you identify the problematic ingredient. From there, find healthier alternatives so you don't feel deprived.

Chlorella: This freshwater algae contains a powerhouse of nutrients that have antimicrobial, anti-tumor, and anti-inflammatory properties. It's often recommended to help with immune system support, respiratory and heart health, and maintenance of regular bowel movements. Its high fiber content promotes the growth of beneficial gut bacteria and swift bowel transit time. You can take it as a supplement or add a powdered version to smoothies and juices. The nutrient also happens to be a good source of vitamins and minerals.

Anti-parasites and anti-yeast: *Parasite problems and yeast overgrowth in humans are extremely common and can manifest in whole-head pain. I have a list of my favorite anti-parasite and anti-yeast supplement products on my website.*

Emotional and psychological trauma can easily manifest in gut dysfunction and colon issues. Research even shows that people who have been diagnosed with irritable bowel syndrome (IBS) are more likely to have experienced more stress and trauma in their life.[11] The current thinking is that trauma "sensitizes the brain and gut," says Dr. Yuri Saito Loftus, a gastroenterologist at the Mayo Clinic in Rochester, Minnesota, who has studied the phenomenon.

In particular, she has found stunning links between childhood traumas—the death of a loved one, a car accident, a house fire, divorce, or physical or mental abuse—and heightened risk for adult IBS. So think about your own life and past traumatic experiences that could be contributing to your gut health and risk for headaches. As noted in the flowchart, there's an emotional release technique I use and teach my patients that I'll detail in Chapter 13. You might want to try it on yourself today!

CHAPTER 12

EDIT YOUR DIET AND ENVIRONMENT

Eat Wisely, Factor in Your Blood Type, and Minimize Exposures

When patients with B-type blood come to see me, as was the case for Elinor, who had daily headaches she thought were caused by a misalignment in her upper back and neck, they are often surprised to hear that their "misalignment" is likely in their diet. I instructed Elinor to stop eating chicken, corn, peanuts, and wheat, which she consumed multiple times a week, and her headaches soon vanished.

This is the same experience I had as someone with B-type blood. I was chasing all the diets trying to find what would work for me and help me sustain my exercise efforts in competitive cycling. My attempts to go vegetarian went bust. My wife, however, who is an A blood type, can thrive on chicken and avocados, but she has to avoid red meat.

When people ask me for the number one thing they can do to end their headaches, other than directly treating a known problem triggering their pain, I dive into my rant about good nutrition attuned to their blood type. Everyone has to eat to sustain life.

Food changes how we think, feel, and function. Now that I've been fanatical about what I eat for forty years, in addition to being so engaged with my patients and their journeys toward a pain-free life, I know a thing or two about what constitutes a healthy, headache-free meal and which ingredients can be problematic for a great majority of people.

> *Food is so much more than a source of energy and sustenance. It's also an important "language" for the body to interpret and affect how we think, feel, and function.*

I'm a big believer in the power of nutrition and in synching your dietary choices with your biology, including your blood type. But first, let me give you some general guidelines to help you build the right framework for your eating plan going forward. I'll share my insights about blood type and tell you how you can minimize environmental exposures that could be exaggerating your risk for headaches.

LISTEN TO YOUR BODY

First things first: Remember that every muscle has an associated organ or gland linked to it through a meridian. The body itself is one giant, complex energy system. Our meridians, of which there are twelve primary ones, connect and affect the function of twelve major organs and systems. Examples include the heart and small intestine, the liver and gallbladder, and the lung and colon.

Remember that the body is speaking to you when you feel pain. Pain would not exist if everything in your body were operating perfectly with its highly interconnected systems and collaborations among organs, tissues, cells, and even those parts that are technically not you—your microbiome. Learn to listen to what your body is screaming out to you when pain hits. There's a lot you can do just by stopping to evaluate where you feel weakness or pain. Pain in the back of the neck? Yeast overgrowth. Pain behind the knee? Gallbladder issue. Pain in the front side of the neck? Thyroid issue. Pain below the shoulder blades? Stomach issue.

> *Never forget that pain is a messenger—a teacher of sorts. When pain or a weakness develops, take a moment to stop and evaluate what could be fueling it. Tune in to your body and let it speak to you. See if you can listen to your body's signals routinely as you would listen to anything else going on around you.*

Hopefully you've used the checklists in Part II to match sources of your pain with organs or glands and the location of your headache. Use that as your guide to question and scrutinize what you're doing in life to fuel the pain. Just take a moment to think about where you are feeling off and see if you can find the parallels that I see in my practice. Don't rule out emotional aspects to pain too! Although emotions are not as tangible as your gut or thyroid, emotions can indeed factor into and create physical pain. Recall the analogy: You can't "see" torrential wind, but you can see its impact on structures and the environment.

The body is an immensely interconnected superorganism, as we've been discussing. And it's full of wisdom that's been in development for millions of years. Few people tune in to their body's cues on a regular basis as they go about their days performing mundane tasks and fulfilling commitments and duties. We can easily brush off those minor aches and pains...*until* they accumulate to the point we need to pay attention because they disrupt everyday life and our ability to perform tasks. Note that tuning in to your body should be a *routine habit*, not something reserved for when pain surfaces. The more you listen, the more knowledge you stand to gain about yourself to then prevent future pain.

GO LOW SUGAR AND GLYPHOSATE-FREE

This message is on repeat by now. Reducing your amount of sugar intake will go a long way to help you uplevel your physiology, all the way down to the expression of your genes. You'd be surprised how much sugar lands in unsuspecting food products, such as dressings, soups, condiments, sauces, energy and cereal/protein bars, breads (including multigrain), instant oatmeal, breakfast cereals, granola bars, nut butters, baked beans, sports drinks, and yogurts.

Unless you're paying close attention to what you put in your mouth, you may not have a clue as to how much sugar you're consuming on a daily basis. And if your diet contains a lot of meals that you're not making yourself from scratch, where you can control your ingredients, you're probably eating a level of sugar that would shock you. Our modern food supply is remarkable, but it produces a lot of irresistible junk that keeps us coming back for more. You can get so used to the taste of sugar that you no longer detect sweetness in foods you wouldn't think contain sugar.

> *Sugar leaches zinc. As zinc levels go down, we need more sugar to make our food "taste good."*

Commercial pasta sauce and loaves of whole grain organic bread can be loaded with sugar, but your taste buds are accustomed to it. No joke: Some breads have more sugar than candy! And yes, organic varieties can be labeled as organic if they are made with sugar from organically grown sugarcane or sugar beet plants. Bottom line: *Organic does not equate with healthy or low sugar.*

As an example, one brand of bread has a label that seemingly screams healthy: "Whole Grains, Oatnut Bread, No Artificial Colors or Fillers, No High-Fructose Corn Syrup." But a sandwich made with this loaf will load you up with more sugar than a Hershey's Kiss.

You know you're eating sugar when you bite into a candy bar, but you may not notice the sugar added to your favorite peanut butter spread. In fact, when food manufacturers create "reduced fat" or "diet" versions of their products, they typically replace the fat with sugar. Focus on whole, real foods found around the perimeter of your grocery store (not in the middle aisles where all the packaged goods are kept). Real foods often don't come with nutrition labels. And if they do, your grandmother would recognize the ingredients.

Going glyphosate-free will also help you avoid exposure to this toxic herbicide that will wreak havoc on your physiology and trigger all kinds of headaches (pun intended). Although eating natural sugars found in fruits and vegetables is perfectly fine, it's important to choose organic when possible to reduce glyphosate exposure. Products made with wheat, corn, soy, and inorganic oats should also be limited or avoided (and often these are highly processed anyhow with other unwanted ingredients). Studies have found that eating all-organic for six days can reduce a body's glyphosate load by a whopping 70 percent.[1] So yes, what you put in your mouth matters.

As the old saying goes, you are what you eat. By choosing organic, you maximize opportunities to consume more natural minerals and vitamins—nutrients that your body needs to protect that intestinal lining and balance certain hormones and substances, like stomach acid. The data from studies show that organically grown crops contain more vitamins, minerals, and antioxidants, as well as lower levels of toxic metals and pesticides than "conventionally grown" crops.[2] And I'll add that organic dairy and meat have been shown to contain about 50 percent more omega-3 fatty acids than inorganic dairy and meat.[3]

Here are some additional tips to consider:

- Limit or nix bagels, pastries, donuts, chips, baked desserts, candy, cereals, muffins, and bars.
- Avoid sodas and sweetened beverages, including "diet" varieties with artificial sweeteners. Be mindful of those sugar bombs at the coffee shop and juice bars.
- Look out for other names for sugar: agave nectar, brown sugar, cane crystals, cane sugar, caramel, corn sweetener, corn syrup, high-fructose corn syrup, crystalline fructose, dextrose, evaporated cane juice, fructose, fruit juice, fruit juice concentrates, glucose, golden syrup, honey, inverted sugar, lactose, maltodextrin, maltose, malt syrup, molasses, raw sugar, refiner's sugar, rice syrup, sucrose, and syrup. According to Dr. Robert Lustig, a prominent endocrinologist and best-selling author of *Metabolical*, there are 56 names for sugar. (He keeps a lot of terrific information on his website at www.RobertLustig.com, including a full list of names for sugar.)
- Watch out for partially hydrogenated oils, which are unhealthy trans fats that will raise your bad (LDL) cholesterol and lower your good (HDL) cholesterol. These fats are not as prevalent in the food supply today as in previous years, but they still end up in a lot of

our food products, such as baked goods, fried foods, margarines, and other processed foods. They are often found in foods that have a long shelf life. They also can have a long life in your body. Trans fat can take 120 days to get metabolized, and some experts say it could take up to a year. We don't have enzymes to recognize them, so they sit and muck up the areas where good fats should be binding up.

- Go organic whenever possible in the produce section. At the very least, avoid produce that's on the Environmental Working Group's "Dirty Dozen" list, published each year and available at www.ewg.org. This list is based on U.S. Department of Agriculture findings of conventionally grown foods most likely to contain pesticide residues: strawberries, spinach, kale/collard and mustard greens, peaches, pears, nectarines, apples, grapes, bell and hot peppers, cherries, blueberries, and green beans. Fruits and vegetables with thicker skins that protect the inner flesh tend to have fewer pesticide residues, and all the better if you can peel them (e.g., bananas, avocados). The EWG keeps another list of foods called the Clean 15: avocados, sweet corn, pineapple, onions, papaya, sweet peas, asparagus, honeydew melon, kiwi, cabbage, mushrooms, mangoes, sweet potatoes, watermelon, and carrots.

A note about artificial sugars: You're not doing yourself a favor by consuming sugar substitutes like aspartame and saccharin. Although we used to think these chemicals were inert and didn't affect our biology, studies show the absolute opposite with one landmark 2014 paper in the respected journal *Nature* that set the record straight: Artificial sweeteners adversely alter the microbes in your gut microbiome in ways that lead to metabolic dysfunction.

In other words, these chemicals don't prevent insulin resistance and diabetes—*they may cause them!*

Unfortunately, my mom, Sue, always had a diet soda with her. We had the aspartame discussion many times over the 40-plus years she massively consumed it. I constantly worried about the artificial sweetener's effects on her brain, digestion, and kidneys. That discussion could not overcome the "zero-calorie" diet lifestyle that had so aggressively indoctrinated her. When she died in early 2024, her listed causes of death were heart, lung, and kidney failure complicated by brain swelling. Coincidence?

GO FOR HIGH-QUALITY FATS

The polyunsaturated fats omega-3 fatty acids are the star fats we would do well to consume regularly. These fats are found in cold-water fishes (like salmon and anchovies), flaxseed, and certain nuts (such as walnuts). We tend to under-consume omega-3s and over-consume processed omega-6s, which happen to be a top source of fat in the American diet. Omega-6s, found in a lot of processed foods, will slow your bowel function, whereas omega-3s will enhance it. By focusing on more omega-3s and less omega-6s, you'll move away from that ultra-processed junk. Here's my list of high-quality fat sources:

- Fish (e.g., salmon, tuna, mackerel, anchovies, halibut, sardines, trout, herring) – For a list of sustainably caught fish that contain the lowest amounts of toxins (such as mercury), visit the Monterey Bay Aquarium's Seafood Watch (www.seafoodwatch.org). In some instances, farmed can be cleaner than wild. And for those who don't eat fish, you may want to supplement with a high-quality fish oil.
- Olive, avocado, sesame, and safflower oils

- Flaxseed, hemp seeds, and chia seeds
- Pastured eggs or omega-3-enriched eggs
- Meats and dairy from grass-fed animals (again, organic meats and dairy are ideal)
- Vegetables such as spinach and Brussels sprouts
- Some nuts (and their oils), such as walnuts, almonds, and macadamias

If you're among the millions of people who suffer from chronic constipation, increasing your omega-3 fat intake could be the ticket to bowel success. Chronic constipation is epidemic today and often related to headband headaches. One recent study found that 93 percent of Americans experience occasional constipation, and an astounding 43 percent have it "often" or "all the time." Could that be due to our love of processed, omega-6-filled junk? I think so.

Chronic constipation is epidemic today, affecting millions of Americans. Not only is the condition often related to headband headaches, but it has been linked with inflammation, anxiety, depression, and, most recently, cognitive decline. One recent study in particular showed that chronic constipation, defined as having a bowel movement only every three or more days, is associated with a 73 percent higher risk of cognitive decline.[4] Get things moving again with more fiber, more movement, and more omega-3 fats (and less processed foods high in omega-6).

FACTOR IN YOUR BLOOD TYPE

According to acclaimed naturopathic physician Dr. Peter J. D'Adamo, author of the mega-best-selling *Eat Right for Your Type*, your blood type can affect how you digest and metabolize food.[5] So, if you eat based on your type—avoiding foods that can react chemically with your blood type—you will optimize your body's innate machinery, digest food more efficiently, and prevent triggering pathways that can lead to disease, pain, and headaches. You'll also manage weight more easily, enjoy more energy, and prevent illness in general.

I have leaned into the blood type diet for decades, and so have my patients through my recommendations. Although the documented science remains mixed and no two individuals with the same blood type will experience the same effects, there's no harm in seeing if limiting certain foods based on your type and increasing the "beneficial" foods helps you to end the pain. Think of it as an extra strategy to have in your toolbox.

I'll admit that I was a skeptic myself about blood type diets. But I soon realized that every time I ate an "avoid" food for B-type individuals, I experienced symptoms. Currently, the Blood Type Diet app, which you can download for a few bucks from Google Play or the Apple Store, is a great resource as a form of biofeedback.[6] When you feel low energy, sugar cravings, or an immune crash after eating, use the app to determine what food you just ate that is listed as an "avoid" food for your blood type. Having this understanding will inspire you to change. It is far easier to make positive changes when the consequence of bad choices is understood. It's no longer *"I can't eat this,"* as the decision morphs into *"It is not worth eating that."*

What speaks to me about this dietary approach is the relationship between what you consume and your immune system. This is personalized nutrition, much like other forms of personalized medicine. You see, at the core of this "blood type" science is how your body's immune system functions and works for or against you in response to exposures. As such, I sometimes have referred to the blood type diet as an "immune type diet." Indeed, what you put in your mouth ultimately stirs chemical reactions between those contents, your blood, and your entire immune system. A classic, extreme example is to think of someone who is highly allergic to peanuts. At the mere sniff of a peanut, their body's immune system goes into attack mode and launches a campaign that can end in anaphylactic shock.

Your immune system is smart. It knows how to recognize "self" antigens from "non-self," but sometimes it can get confused and trigger unnecessary reactions to inputs. This is the basis for autoimmunity, whereby the body mistakenly attacks its own tissues. People who are sensitive to gluten, for example, can trigger an attack on their thyroid if they consume gluten-containing wheat, whose protein, gliadin, resembles an enzyme of the thyroid. This cascade of events is technically called molecular mimicry. As the body launches an attack against the gliadin protein, which resembles, or "mimics," the same protein sequences found in the thyroid, the thyroid becomes a target too as the immune system falls prey to mistaken identity.

BLOOD TYPE APPLICATIONS

Let's go a little further into blood type science without getting too technical. There are dozens of blood types, though most people are familiar with one of the main four groups: A, B, AB, and O. The presence or absence of two antigens found on the surface of your red blood cells determines which type you are. Antigens are simply substances that can trigger an immune response if they are foreign to the body. Whatever antigen you carry on your blood cells is linked with the antibodies in your plasma. Antibodies are proteins in your immune system that police the system and attack foreign substances that could be harmful.

If you carry only the A antigen on your red blood cells, then you are blood type A, and you also make anti-B antibodies. You would not be able to receive type B or AB blood due to the mismatch and the body's reaction to any donor blood with the B antigen. If you carry only the B antigen, then you are blood type B with anti-A antibodies ready to incite a reaction to any encounters with type A or AB blood. If you carry both, you're AB (and can receive transfusions from any blood type). And if you don't have either A or B, you're O type with both anti-A and anti-B antibodies, so you can only receive O-type blood but can be a universal donor. Blood type is passed down genetically. The key thing to remember is that your unique blood type determines how your immune system responds to incoming substances.

Now, let's take this one step further. You may have heard about lectins before, as they have been in the media recently and are affiliated with certain diets. Lectins are a large family of proteins that are found throughout the food kingdom but are especially common in grains, legumes, and nightshade vegetables, such as eggplants, tomatoes, and potatoes. They have glue-like properties that affect your blood and the lining of your digestive tract. In the body, lectins bind to carbohydrates to form larger molecules called *glycoproteins*, which perform many functions within the body— from regulating the immune system to keeping protein levels in the blood under control.

There are good and bad lectins, the latter of which you want to avoid. Many lectins are, in fact, beneficial and aid in your biology when they agree with your blood type. When you eat food containing lectins that are incompatible with your blood type, the lectins target an organ or bodily system and can begin to interact with the tissues in that area. Most lectins are harmless, and many are rendered inactive through cooking methods or can be neutralized by the presence of good lectins.

BLOOD TYPE KEY PLAYERS

Here's your cheat sheet to know what you should be avoiding based on your blood type:

O Type (the most common type, about 44 percent of people in the U.S.)

- Reduce or avoid: corn, coffee, grains (especially wheat and wheat products), peanuts, dairy, soybean oil, kidney beans
- Go light on: beans, legumes, eggs
- A-okay: animal proteins (e.g., beef, poultry, fish), vegetables

> **TIP:** Beef is like medicine for the O type (you will struggle if you're a vegetarian). Order beef, tuna, and eggs. O types tend to have stronger stomachs but are prone to ulcers. O types often need good sources of methionine to drive that methylation pathway, thereby reducing the effects of bad genes, preventing cancer, stabilizing blood sugar, and supporting detoxification. If you're not going to eat meat, take methionine as a supplement.

Ideal exercise: Try vigorous, high-intensity training.

A Type (roughly 42 percent of Americans)

- Reduce or avoid: red meat (aim for a meat-free diet, with the exception of poultry), dairy (especially milk), wheat, corn, lima and kidney beans, tomatoes, eggplant, chickpeas

- A-okay: fruits (including avocados), vegetables, fish, beans, legumes (including peanuts), whole gluten-free grains (ideally fresh and organic Ezekiel)

> **TIP:** Fish and poultry are excellent sources of protein for A types who struggle with beef and are prone to low stomach acid, high cortisol, and intestinal problems. When you crave breads, seek Ezekiel sprouted varieties that are easily digested and also provide all the essential amino acids your body needs.

Ideal exercise: Go for low-impact, yoga-type exercises that are calming and centering.

B Type (about 14 percent of Americans)

- Reduce or avoid: tomatoes, corn, wheat, soy, chicken, peanuts, avocados, lentils
- A-okay: green vegetables, fruits, eggs, fish, low-fat dairy (especially cultured dairy products), certain meats

> **TIP:** Lamb, turkey, and wild-caught salmon are superfood sources of protein for B types.

Ideal exercise: B types are nonconformists (I'm one!), so we need diversity in our activities.

AB Type (the least common type, only about 4 percent of the U.S. population)

- Reduce or avoid: beef, smoked or cured meats, chicken, corn, caffeine, alcohol, fava beans, bananas

- A-okay: fish, dairy (especially cultured dairy products), green vegetables, tofu

 TIP: Turkey and lamb are superfood sources of protein.

Ideal exercise: Like B types, ABs also need diversity, a combination of high- and low-intensity activities.

Note: Pork can be problematic for all blood types. Pork can inhibit the immune system and slow digestion. According to Dr. D'Adamo, signs of problems with dietary lectins include the following: bloating or gas after meals, unexplained fatigue, changes in bowel habits, achy joints and muscles, hormonal imbalances, and skin eruptions. Look out for an energy crash after a meal or an immune strain, as evidenced by sinus congestion or throat irritation.

MINIMIZE EXPOSURES

The number of chemicals we're exposed to on a daily basis is mind-boggling. As dwellers of an industrialized nation, we harbor hundreds of synthetic chemicals in our bodies from food, air, and water. Our reliance on plastics is one of the largest sources of chemicals that wind up in our environment—and in our bodies. Some of these chemicals have the power to interrupt our hormonal system and are deemed *endocrine-disrupting chemicals*, or EDCs. It doesn't help that many industries that produce chemical-laden products, such as the beauty and cosmetic industry, are not well regulated. It behooves us to take control of our exposures so we can reduce the risk of damage to our biology that can manifest in headaches.

In addition to rethinking what you eat, think about what consumer products you bring home, from personal care products to what you clean your home with, how you furnish and decorate your home, and even how you tend to your garden. You don't have to panic at the thought of throwing everything out and starting afresh, and not every synthetic chemical is bad or harmful. But do start to think about what's around you and how you can minimize potentially harmful ingredients. Here are some tips to consider:

- **Clean feet**: We trudge through all kinds of stuff while walking outside, from pesticides and herbicides to petroleum products and dog poop. If you're not one who takes their shoes off at the front door when you get home, think about making a habit of doing that with your family members. You can toss them in a nearby closet, buy an inexpensive shoe rack, or simply keep a large basket or other container by the front door.

- **Clean hands**: We got used to hand-washing during the COVID pandemic. Don't neglect this important habit that only needs plain soap and water. You'll prevent the transfer of toxins from all over into your body through the mouth, eyes, and nose. Note that most hand sanitizers are another source of chemical toxins. If you are going to use a hand sanitizer, choose a clean plant-based version or an essential oil.

- **Clean skin**: We love our toiletries and beauty and personal care products—perfumes, hair sprays and gels, body lotions, shampoos, and makeup. But these products can be loaded with chemicals, many of which can be absorbed through the skin and go directly into the bloodstream. Chemicals can also enter the body through other routes. You don't have to run out and replace all your products with safer organic alternatives, but as you buy products in the future, think about switching your brands. For guidance, check out the Environmental Working Group's Skin Deep® database, which offers a lot of information and resources. Also, keep in mind that organic skincare products can be irritating too.

- **Clean air**: Household air can become more toxic than what's outside as household dust, dirt, gasses, mold, and mildew accumulate. To keep your breathing space as pure as possible, consider using a vacuum with a HEPA filter. HEPA stands for *high-efficiency particulate air*. To qualify as a HEPA filter, the product must remove 99.97 percent of airborne particles measuring 0.3 microns or greater in diameter passing through them. You can also consider adding HEPA air purifiers to rooms that you spend a lot of time in, like the kitchen, den, bedrooms, and home office. Minimize the use of fragrant candles and air "fresheners." Although urban dwellers may think they have it worse than rural residents due to thicker air pollution, people who live far from traffic and airports may be surprised by what lurks from local farms and manufacturing plants.

- **Clean water**: What's in your water? You can find out by going to the EWG's Tap Water Database (www.ewg.org/tapwater/) and punching in your ZIP code. Use a water filtration system at home for drinking and cooking, and it doesn't have to be fancy. A variety of water treatment technologies are available today, from simple and inexpensive water filtration pitchers you fill manually to under-the-sink systems and whole-house filters that will filter all the water coming into your home from its source. Note that in 2023, an alarming study came out showing that bottled water is full of plastic particles that could be harmful to your health.[7] A liter of bottled water can contain nearly a quarter of a million pieces of "nanoplastics," which are pieces of plastic so small you cannot see them, as they are smaller than the size of a single speck of household dust. Filtered tap water is better than bottled water, but carry your water in stainless steel or glass bottles rather than plastic.

- **Clean household goods**: No need to remodel and refurbish your home, but the next time you're in the market for new bedding, furniture, and flooring, aim to buy products made with more natural ingredients and fabrics. Carpets, for example, can "off-gas" chemicals for years and affect sensitive people. Although many of these goods, such as mattresses, upholstered furniture, and children's products, are required by law to have fire retardants (FRs) in them, FRs are increasingly being regulated, and less toxic goods are coming on the market. When buying cleaning products, choose eco-friendly, green alternatives to harsh chemicals.

> *Among the most common toxins in everyday commercial goods—from building materials and household products (flooring, furniture, upholstery) to cosmetics and detergents—are aldehydes, notably formaldehyde. If you find you are sensitive to these products, and especially if mosquitoes also like you, you may do well to take a good B1 (thiamine) product. Go to HeadacheAdvantage.com to find some recommendations.*

- **Clean garden**: Switch from traditional herbicides and pesticides to non-toxic, organic varieties. Bonus: Grow and maintain a garden of seasonal fruits and vegetables in rich organic soil. You'll know where your produce comes from!

Finally, see if you can purge some of the plastic in your life. Store food in ceramic or glass rather than plastic. Bring your own reusable, non-plastic grocery bags and containers to avoid single-use items. See if you can move away from disposable plastics such as cutlery, coffee cup lids, and plastic wrap, and never microwave plastic! Fully 90 percent of the plastic items in our daily lives are only used once, and many of them end up in precious waterways and oceans. If you start to make small shifts in your plastic usage, you'll be doing yourself—and the planet—a favor.

CHAPTER 13

ALLOW FOR SLEEP, EXERCISE, AND STRESS REDUCTION

How to Find Balance in Life

As I was beginning to put this chapter together, a new Gallup Panel report came out stating that we've veered away from healthy habits since the beginning of the pandemic.[1] Our health has plummeted as obesity and diabetes have reached record highs. Unfortunately, sugar, caffeine, and MSG exaggerate the stress response. By the end of the day, 90 percent of people feel some degree of stress.[2] That might not seem too surprising, but get this: Over a quarter (28 percent) of people surveyed claimed to feel stressed "all the time" or "often" after their day is done. It doesn't have to be that way. It *shouldn't* be that way.

Stress is a normal part of life, and we do need it. Just the right amount of good stress, what's called *eustress*, can be motivating and invigorating. It will keep you alert, energized, attentive, creative, optimistic, and moving forward. It gets your blood running, positively stimulates your immune system, and supports healthy hormone balance. In fact, good stress will *increase* the feel-good hormone (dopamine) so you feel pleasure in response to stressful experiences. New research in the past few years has changed how we now think about this important hormone and neurotransmitter key to the central nervous system.[3] Under the right circumstances, it's critical for our mental wellbeing, but under other circumstances, it can be associated with dysfunctions in processing emotions, cognitive activities, and even pain.

Too much stress can creep into unhealthy territory. On a scale of 1 to 10, how would you rate your stress levels? Are they off the charts (over 10), or can you keep them steady and below a 5? What keeps you up at night? How would you rate your overall habits and their effects on your vitality?

I've already given you lots to think about in terms of reshaping your diet, but there's a lot more to the equation of health. I routinely ask my patients about their sleep, their attempts to decompress, and their fitness habits. Many of them admit to restless nights, chronic sleep deprivation, lack of time or energy for exercise, and no real strategies for coping with toxic stress. Some have emotional baggage and past traumas that are most definitely weighing into their headaches.

Emotions don't just wreak havoc on our minds, but they in fact can have physical impacts on our bodies. If that weren't true, then we wouldn't be able to document clear relationships between the experience of psychological "pain" and real physical pain. Ancient Chinese medicine has long respected the connection between emotions and certain glands and organs, much in the way we've been discussing the links between muscles and other tissues. Scientific research is catching up with antiquity, proving that certain parts of our bodies are indeed connected to emotions.

According to ancient wisdom, grief and sadness are felt in the lungs, skin, and large intestine; hence, you experience that tightness in the chest when overwhelmed with sorrow. Fear affects the kidneys, ears, and bladder; hence, you may feel the urge to pee when facing a sudden fight-or-flight situation. Anxiety is felt in the stomach, pancreas, and spleen; hence, the nausea and upset stomach when stressed out to the max. Positive emotions also have ties to organs, such as trust and the gut, love and the heart, and pride and the lungs. But positive emotions are not going to give you a headache. It's the negative feelings that can be so disruptive to our normal physiology.

In this chapter, I'm going to cover the three big buckets of additional habits to address that will hopefully help you dial down your stress. You cannot enhance your physical health without addressing your emotional health. This will include strategies for releasing negative emotions that could be "sitting" in an organ or gland, rendering it weak and contributing to headaches. You may not even know it, but that argument you had last month with a loved one or that car accident you had a few years ago could be doing more damage to your actual biology than you can imagine.

If you were to be in my exam room right now, I'd start by addressing any structural problems your body may be experiencing, then I'd move to your dietary and supplement needs, and lastly, I'd see if there are emotional corrections to be made. We'd work together to release tension in the body held from past trauma that causes pain—and headaches. There's a simple technique, which I'll explain in this chapter, that you can try on yourself to help you release your own emotional tensions. And it only takes a minute!

But first, let's take a tour of the best balancing tools of life: sleep, exercise, and "rest during waking hours." If you don't gain control of these vital aspects of a balanced body, you won't gain control of your headaches!

SLEEP THE PAIN AWAY

You may not have viewed sleep as medicine before, but it's one of the only "drugs" shown to have direct and indirect effects on physical and emotional health.[4] The scientific evidence speaks

The body craves balance and regularity, what's called *homeostasis*. In a homeostatic state, your body fires on all cylinders and maintains balance across its systems, including those all-important hormonal ones. And one of the easiest ways to ensure homeostasis is by getting regular high-quality sleep

volumes: High-quality sleep has immense effects on metabolism and related hormones that control appetite, satiety, and weight. Sleep also has a big impact on our inner clock that manages those hormones and our sense of day versus night, or what's called our *circadian rhythm*. In the pain department, poor sleep is well documented in the scientific literature to be a risk factor for the development of chronic pain. In the headache realm, sleep disorders or poor sleep and headaches are also well documented to be paired together.

You know that your body yearns for balance and regularity. When your sleep schedule is thrown off, you feel it in your physicality and in your mood. The impairments that occur with sleep deprivation have even been shown in studies to parallel impairments due to alcohol intoxication. Being awake for seventeen hours, for instance, is similar to having a blood-alcohol concentration (BAC) of 0.05 percent, which is the cut-off for driving purposes in many countries (it's 0.08 percent in the U.S.). Twenty-four hours of being awake will make you "drunk"—the equivalent of a 0.10 percent BAC! When you're sleep-deprived, the body is not on even keel, and its systems, including many hormonally controlled ones, are not optimized for full functionality. Suffice it to say, if you can maintain healthy sleep habits, you can protect your body's homeostatic state and keep its firing of hormones on cue. Following are the top three tips:

Know your number: What amount of sleep makes you feel rested and ready for the day? Not many people can get by with fewer than five hours, and those who do are usually fooling themselves. Most of us need between seven and nine hours a night. Although quality of sleep trumps quantity, you do have a number of hours that plays into that quality. If you don't bank enough restorative slow-wave sleep in a single night, you won't have all of your cylinders firing the next day.

Keep it consistent: No more sleeping in on the weekends. Just kidding! Well, you can try to make up for a sleep deficit on a day off from work, but your body will suffer as its circadian rhythm is thrown off. Aim to go to bed and rise at the same time daily, weekends and holidays included. If you disrupt your rhythm, you disrupt your body's normal physiology, including the ebb and flow of hormonal secretions. Your metabolism will likewise take a hit. Be consistent with your bedtime routine too. Within an hour of bedtime, stop performing stimulating or stressful tasks and engage in an activity that signals to your body that it's almost time to sleep. Examples include reading, listening to music, and taking a warm bath.

Keep it cool, quiet, and dark: The ideal temperature for sleep is between 60 and 70°F. You want to maintain a bedroom that's clutter-

Don't know your magic number of hours to feel fully rested and ready to go the next day? On your next day off, go to bed at your regular time and see what time you wake up naturally the next morning without an alarm. Be sure you have no distractions at night caused by light or noise.

No-no's in the bedroom at night: cell phones, tablets, laptops, and any other light-emitting electronics. If you have a television in your bedroom that you watch late at night, be extra cautious about how its stimulating light could be affecting your sleep (and your bedtime!).

free, quiet, and pitch-black dark. Consider using blackout curtains on your windows and a white noise machine to cancel out the sounds outside. That darkness stimulates melatonin in the brain to not only support sleep but also help heal the brain and prepare it for the next day of activity. As the light hits light sensors in the retina of your eye, a message gets sent to the suprachiasmatic nerve in the hypothalamus, which you'll recall is a master coordinator of many bodily functions and controls many of the autonomic functions of the body, especially metabolism. The hypothalamus links the nervous and endocrine systems, and when it receives input from your eyes, it synchronizes your body clock with the 24-hour day, thereby "resetting" your circadian clock.

If you continue to fail at getting a good night's rest, you may want to undergo a sleep study to rule out other issues. You may, for example, have a sleep disorder such as sleep apnea, a condition that affects millions of Americans. The disorder is caused by a collapse of the airway during sleep as muscles in the back of the throat fail to keep the airway open. This makes the sleeper stop breathing briefly until the body reflexively responds in a semi-awake state. Then the cycle repeats, causing fragmented overall sleep.

The telltale signs of sleep apnea are dreamless sleep and loud snoring. The most common cause of the disorder? *Obesity*, as that extra weight and fat around the neck create a setting that triggers the airway collapse. Sleep apnea can be treated with the help of a continuous positive airway pressure (CPAP) device, but the best solution is weight loss.

Believe it or not, it actually takes energy to sleep and properly restore. When the adrenals are fatigued and blood sugar is unstable, you're more prone to sleep disorders, snoring, and weight gain. I once had a young engaged patient who was very nervous about her upcoming sleeping arrangements because she could hear her fiancé's snoring two rooms away. As a wedding gift, I gave the couple a bottle of vitamins containing glycine to help support blood sugar balance. She vehemently shared with me that the supplements were the most valuable and appreciated of all their wedding gifts. They are now happily married and both are sleeping soundly.

MOVE THE PAIN OUT

I love my exercise. Even on my busiest days, I make time to get my workout in. I mix up the intensity of my workouts throughout the week, varying the type of bicycling between my road and mountain bikes in the great outdoors, where I can commune with nature. And I also do some upper body and core strength training to complete the picture.

I'm not the first person to tell you that exercise does a body good. There is no end to the number of studies showing how exercise positively impacts the body all the way down to its genomic expression or how your genes behave and play into pain biology. It just may be the only thing we can do that lowers our risk of death from all causes. It also makes us massively more productive and energetic. When you power up a hill on a bike, take an aerobics class, or play a team sport at the local rec center, your entire physiology changes for the better. Spend a mere thirty minutes moving at an intensity that gets your heart pumping and you'll be twice as effective in your work the rest of the day and lower your risk for a headache. Among the top ten benefits of exercise that have everything to do with the risk of headaches are the following:

- Blood sugar balance and lower risk of insulin resistance, diabetes, and obesity
- Increased blood flow and lymph circulation, which means more oxygen going to your cells and tissues, and increased heart and immune health
- Stronger muscles and bones
- Lower risk of developing metabolic syndromes (e.g., high blood pressure, high cholesterol)
- Increase in the release of endorphins that act as natural mood lifters and pain relievers
- Decreased inflammation
- Better, deeper, and more restorative sleep
- Enhanced ability to achieve and maintain an ideal weight
- Greater stamina, coordination, and flexibility
- Stress reduction, increased self-esteem, and sense of wellbeing

The headlines you read a few years ago are true: Prolonged sitting can be worse than smoking. Studies began to emerge in 2010 showing that prolonged sitting busts metabolic health, and no matter your age, body weight, or amount of physical activity, too much sitting increases the risk of premature death.[5]

The research highlighted the fact that we cannot necessarily make up for sitting all day with a power-hour run at lunch. Your metabolism demands regular movement. When you are relatively immobile, your circulation slows down and your body uses less of your blood sugar. In particular, the volume of blood plasma alone circulating in your body decreases after a few days of inactivity. In addition to adverse effects on blood fats and hormone balance, sedentariness will bomb your resting blood pressure and metabolic rate and imprison your muscles—putting them into a sort of dormant state where their electrical activity is diminished. Just twelve days of inactivity can lead to a dramatic decrease in the amount of blood pumping and its delivery of precious oxygen to cells.

My hope is you can establish a fitness routine that works for you if you don't already maintain one. Find an activity you truly enjoy, which will vastly improve sustainability. If you are already consistent with a routine, keep it going! Think about enlisting an exercise/accountability buddy who could also benefit from your wonderful discipline.

A well-rounded exercise program includes a blend of cardio work, strength training, and stretching. Refer back to pages 164–166 to remind yourself of precisely which types of exercise could best match your blood type. As I said, I need diversity with some intensity, but you may do better with forms of exercise that are more yoga-like in nature and calming to your nervous system.

You can get a dose of cardio, strength training, and stretching with virtually any type of exercise. And the benefits are often cumulative. You can engage in short bursts of exercise throughout the day or commit to a routine that sets aside an hour or so. If you

> Your body's metabolism *requires* regular movement. Physical activity affects every cell in your body. Without regular movement, cells don't perform as optimally, and systems stall.

do pack the majority of your exercise into a single time period during your day, however, be sure to avoid sitting the rest of the day. Choose the stairs instead of the elevator, park farther away from your destination, and try a standing desk if you have a desk job. Here are some additional tips:

- Move for at least two minutes every hour (get off that seat!) and take movement breaks throughout the day to have "exercise snacks." Use alarms if you need reminders.
- Do some stretching and weight-bearing exercises when you watch TV.
- Find online fitness programs to follow from the comfort of your home.
- Don't get bored with your routine. Surprise your body and challenge its muscles in different ways by switching up the activities you choose. In addition to focusing on cardio and strength, think about working on balance and coordination.
- Take advantage of apps to track your movement.

There's no excuse these days for dodging exercise. With the volume of opportunities out there accessible via the internet and your smartphone, you don't have to buy into a gym membership. Do what you can to get your heart rate up for at least thirty minutes a day at a minimum, ideally an hour. Get the blood moving and everything about you will be better. If you have been sedentary for a while, ease into a routine. Start with walks around your neighborhood and then increase the time, speed, and intensity as your body adapts to this new lifestyle change. Muscles retain memories from previous fitness levels, so you can make a bounce back to being in shape faster. Some experts say you can regain about one-half of your fitness in under two weeks if you engage in moderately hard workouts.

The fitter you become, the more benefits you will gain. Be patient with the transformation and listen to your body as you go. It can take six to eight weeks to notice changes, but you'll reap rewards the first time you push yourself physically that you may not necessarily feel. Stay focused on the big picture.

Exercise not only helps us organize our thoughts, but it also reduces the physical storage of emotions. For example, the famous "runner's high" is literally the result of an increased release of dopamine. There's no better example to prove the power of exercise on the very biochemicals we need to feel good and in control of our emotions.

RELEASE THE EMOTIONAL PAIN

Optimal sleep and movement will go a long way to help you manage stress and emotional "unfitness," but there are other things you could be doing that can further support your sense of wellbeing. I'll venture to guess you've gotten the memo about the benefits of certain stress-reducing strategies like meditation, deep breathing, journaling, and even taking a walk outside in nature, so I won't be going into detail about those methods. I also don't feel the need to cover the importance of socializing, connecting and keeping in touch with loved ones in person, and managing your social media use. Those are all excellent stress management tools.

The key to fitness is to find an activity you love to do that ups your heart rate and challenges your muscles, balance, and coordination. Fit people live longer and have fewer disabilities—and fewer headaches! The fitter you are, the more benefits you gain.

What I'd like to offer is a brief review of lesser-known trends in stress reduction through modalities you may not be as familiar with and which have actually been used by healthcare practitioners like me for decades. At the core of these innovative healing methods is an appreciation for the dynamics of the mind-body connection and the storage of stressful emotions in our body, often at the subconscious level. Virtually every patient I treat has some form of locked trauma, be it a problem with a relationship, issues with finances, a job, bad memories of past accidents, and difficult events in life.

Case in point: I once treated a twelve-year-old boy who had been hit by a car. His mother brought him in for me to make some structural adjustments, and she happened to mention that her son had been a straight-A student before the accident. Now, he was struggling in school and barely passing. On his intake form, I noticed that a doctor thought he was colorblind to blue and green, which didn't make sense to me. When he told me the last two things he remembered from the accident were the green light signal and the blue minivan coming at him that eventually hit him, I knew his problem was an emotional short circuit related to the traumatic memory. I performed a technique called NET (see below) on him to treat those emotions, and he soon began thriving again at school.

I can't recall a patient who did NOT have any emotional trauma locked up inside. We all carry emotional hits from the past or present. But we can respond to them consciously by first acknowledging them and then working on their release so they have less of a physical impact.

You may not be able to perform these techniques all on your own, but you can certainly find trained professionals to help you out or, in some cases, online tutorials. Here are my two favorites:

Neuro-Emotional Technique (NET): Dr. Scott Walker developed NET in the 1980s and began teaching seminars that eventually led to certifying other healthcare practitioners around the world with this innovative technique. The goal of NET is to clear unresolved negative emotions that manifest as physical pain. It helps to clear your mind of worries, fears, and negative beliefs that get in the way of feeling vibrant. Whether you've got pent-up emotions around certain people in your life or issues with yourself like low self-esteem, anger, and conflicts within your career, NET can help release that negative energy.

The technique is based on a collection of principles taught in chiropractic medicine that leverages the power of applied kinesiology, the neuroscience of pain and mind-body dynamics, acupuncture-meridian correlations, the Pavlovian response, and the biology of physiological responses and memory. You can find certified and non-certified practitioners of NET in your geographic area using Dr. Walker's online tool at www.mindbody. com/find-a-practitioner .

One NET technique you can try on your own is one I've developed by combining a few techniques without getting overly complicated. Like traditional NET, it uses pulse points on the wrists associated with various emotional responses. You see, there are three acupressure points on each wrist that can be pressed in a single motion to release physical manifestations of negative emotions. If you know something happened and ever since then you've had regular headaches or some other pain in the body, here's what you can do:

1. Identify the negative issue or event bothering you. It could be a bad memory, like a car accident, the death of a loved one, a disturbing conversation in a fraught relationship, stress over your job, or a difficult child. Think of that moment and put the snapshot of that in your head, even if it's unpleasant to recall. Now take one hand (right or left, doesn't matter) and wrap your fingers around your other wrist, palms up, on the thumb side.
2. Place the hand with the wrapped wrist, palm open, on your forehead and gently tuck your chin down and up while you keep pondering that event.
3. Switch hands and repeat the above steps with the other wrist.

To see this demonstrated by yours truly, go to my website at HeadacheAdvantage.com.

Emotional Freedom Technique (EFT): This technique, which was developed by Gary Craig in the 1990s, is based on meridian points and related to acupressure, but it uses fingertip tapping to stimulate certain points on your hands, face, and body as you focus on your internal fears, uncomfortable feelings, and sources of emotional trauma. The goal is to neutralize those negative feelings with positive affirmations so your brain responds to stressful memories in a neutral way.

EFT draws from a menu of scientific theories beyond acupressure, such as neuro-linguistic programming, cognitive behavioral therapy, and energy medicine. EFT has been used to treat anxiety and post-traumatic stress disorder in war veterans, active military service members, and civilians. Multiple studies have been done on the method over the years and show that it can be very effective. In a recent 2023 study, for instance, EFT was shown to reduce the anxiety and stress that healthcare professionals felt during the pandemic.[6] Another 2022 study found it to be useful in boosting self-esteem among nurses.[7] The research continues, as EFT is now being studied for treating a wide range of conditions, from depression and anxiety to physical pain and even obesity. You can learn more about EFT at www.emofree.com. You can find a clinical EFT practitioner through EFT International (https://eftinternational.org).

As humans, we are deeply emotional beings and creatures of habit. Our emotions and habits often go hand in hand, as how we feel drives our behaviors and the decisions we make. Suppressing our negative emotions will work against us and eventually spill out in unwanted ways, which can include unrelenting headaches. Give yourself permission to process your emotions—even the toughest ones, like shame, anger, fear, anxiety, sadness, and grief—and find the right healing journey that allows you to minimize their impact on your mind and body.

CHAPTER 14

DEDICATE
(AND TROUBLESHOOT)

Q&A

*C*ongratulations! You've no doubt learned a lot in this book and have charted a new course in your lifestyle to minimize the number and intensity of your headaches. Perhaps you've managed to get rid of them entirely! As with so many things in life, staying healthy and pain-free demands an ongoing commitment to healthy habits. Every day, you're up against new challenges, but you're also faced with opportunities to do better and make good decisions that will play into your health and sense of wellbeing.

Wisdom is the application of knowledge. You have learned to listen better to what your head and body are trying to tell you via pain responses. My hope is you can navigate your path forward with the insights gained from this book and the positive changes you make that have significant effects on your biology. Nobody is perfect, so as you go about your daily life now, focus on progress one step at a time. Enjoy the journey. Celebrate the growth.

In this final chapter, I'm going to answer the top ten questions I get about implementing my strategies and seeking a headache-free life. This will ultimately help you to fully dedicate yourself to the mission here and troubleshoot any problems you encounter. Everyone's experience with headaches will be different. The key is to find what works for you, stick with it, and further improve as your life demands change!

Q. I'm having a hard time figuring out what in my diet is bothering me and giving me headaches. I've eliminated foods not compatible with my blood type. What else can I do?

A. Keep a food journal and be rigorous about paying attention to everything you put in your mouth. In your food journal, make note of when symptoms worsen. This will allow you the opportunity to look backward for common triggers. Be especially mindful of processed and packaged foods you buy that can contain hidden ingredients, especially added sugars and chemical additives. Don't be fooled by products labeled as "organic" or "100% natural," because even those can be deceiving. By recording everything you consume, you'll likely realize how much "mindless eating" goes on in your day-to-day life. And *no cheating!*

If you accept a piece of cake or other treat at your colleague's office birthday party, don't forget to write that down. Also, don't leave out your beverages, even if you think they are harmless. You may have been drinking a popular diet soda for decades and not realized that it could be contributing to your headaches.

Q. Are there medicines that could be causing my headaches?

A. Indeed, the list of medicines that can cause headaches is long and includes both over-the-counter and prescription drugs. Examples include heart and blood pressure medications, pain relievers, statins, proton pump inhibitors, erectile dysfunction drugs, antidepressants, sleeping pills, and hormonal birth control pills.

Even drugs used to *treat* headaches can cause them, such as acetaminophen, ibuprofen, decongestants, aspirin, codeine, triptans, and combination drugs that contain caffeine. Take inventory of all the medicines you take and ask your healthcare provider for alternatives to headache-inducing drugs if possible.

Q. Is there anything I can do to stop an oncoming headache?

A. The moment you feel a headache starting is a great opportunity to sit and think about what might have sparked it. Was it something you ate? Did you indulge in more sugar than usual? Could something you consumed contain MSG (see list on page 54). Did you skip a meal? Is your body off its rhythm from a bad night's sleep? A stressful event or emotional trigger?

Try taking the supplement that best fits your headache pattern in the flowcharts. If it is the right solution for you, you should begin to enjoy relief almost as soon as the vitamin is tasted. This builds profound confidence in the approach. If that supplement doesn't eradicate your headache within a week of beginning it, try the next closest supplemental solution. The answer is in these pages, but it may take some investigation on your part and experimenting with different potential solutions until you find your answer. Trust the process, it works!

Q. I love coffee. I drink a cup or two every morning. How can I wean myself off it and find an alternative?

A. Losing the coffee habit is among the hardest things to do for my patients who would do well to avoid the popular stimulant. People with O blood types in particular should avoid it entirely. Start by switching to a half-decaf, half-regular cup and slowly switch to green tea.

Green tea has caffeine, but it also includes the amino acid threonine. Threonine helps to reduce the side effects of caffeine. Green tea is also considered "highly beneficial" for all four blood types.

Q. What are your thoughts on preventive medications for migraines currently on the market? And is there ever a good time for taking traditional headache medicines like aspirin, ibuprofen, and naproxen sodium (e.g., Aleve)?

A. There is a time and place for these pain-blocking medications, but they typically come with a health compromise, much in the way antibiotics will bomb your microbiome but are necessary for treating acute infections that could be life-threatening, and thus should be reserved for such rare situations. When it comes to common headache medications, including those that are anti-inflammatory, most of these drugs inhibit a liver pathway (called *sulfation*), which then slows detoxification and healing.

You will get the best response and learn the true cause of your headaches by following the flowcharts laid out in this book. Start with the flowchart related to the area in which you most commonly experience headaches. This will likely lead you to a resolution. Note too that chronic use of headache medicines can also contribute to "rebound" headaches, as we discussed earlier. It's a vicious cycle.

Q. I seem to get headaches only on the weekends or when I'm on vacation. Why, and what can I do about it?

A. People who suffer from headaches on "days off" typically disrupt their circadian rhythms by changing their sleep habits temporarily. Keep your sleep schedule the same seven days a week, 365 days a year. Also pay attention to your dietary habits that can also shift on those days off. You may notice, for instance, that you find yourself splurging on too much sugar or alcohol. Your body—including your head—loves consistency and predictability. The closer you can stick to the same schedule daily, the more you lower your risk of a headache.

Q. Is it possible for someone to have multiple types of headaches?

A. Yes! Many of my patients will relieve one type of headache only to encounter another type soon thereafter. Use the checklists and flowcharts in this book to keep sleuthing your way through the process of identifying your headache's characteristics. You may feel like you're playing a game of whack-a-mole, but as you address your body's weaknesses one by one, you'll move closer to the goal of being pain-free and thriving.

Q. I am being treated for a medical condition unrelated to my headaches. What should I be mindful of when implementing these strategies?

A. Don't stop taking any medications your doctor has prescribed for your condition, but do share with your healthcare provider the changes you're making in your diet, supplement regimen, and general lifestyle. Look into possible side effects of the medications you are on. In addition to finding a list of side effects on a drug's packaging and label, you can also search online at places like MedlinePlus.gov, WebMD.com/interaction-checker, and Drugs.com.

Solving your health concerns by working through the flowcharts might also solve the condition you were seeking medical advice for. As you make these changes and enjoy the improved vitality from your enhanced lifestyle, share your experiences with your doctor to see if your prescriptions should change.

Q. My headaches are often accompanied by nausea and light sensitivity. What can I do about that?

A. Nausea is typically associated with a right-sided headache and, therefore, a gallbladder problem. Light sensitivity occurs with adrenal fatigue. Under acute stress, the adrenal gland constricts the pupil to focus on safety. With chronic stress, however, the ability to maintain that constriction gets compromised and cannot hold steady for more than 24 seconds, even when exposed to light. When the pupil (the iris) is unable to maintain proper constriction, incoming light through a dilated pupil becomes irritating (light sensitivity).

I routinely test my patients' pupil responses to light and gain a sense of how their bodies are handling stress. The eyes are indeed a window into the body's autonomic nervous system, which is one of the main neural pathways activated by stress. Hence, you may want to take inventory of your life's stressors and see about turning the volume down so your stress response can normalize and your pupils can pass the contraction test.

Q. When should my head pain be considered a medical emergency?

A. The vast majority of headaches are not reflective of a serious condition. It may feel like you've got a massive brain tumor or are experiencing a stroke, but the chances of those events are extremely low. That said, seek medical help if your headache is accompanied by mental confusion, trouble speaking or seeing, a high fever, fainting, a stiff neck, prolonged vomiting, numbness or paralysis on one side of the body, or trouble walking.

A headache that comes on rather suddenly without any known reason and that seems like the worst headache of your life may call for immediate medical attention. But again, most headaches are not a medical emergency. They may be painful and frustrating, but they are not signs that your life is in danger. When they strike, stop and take a good reality check on other areas bothering you. Think about those emotional inputs as well. Did your sudden headache follow an argument, a bad memory, or stressful news? Chances are, your headache is trying to tell you something. The answers exist.

It is the goal of this book to provide you with the strategies to find those answers. Your diligence and continued pursuit of solutions are your allies. You need to be your best advocate. As you make these seemingly simple changes to your life, pay attention to how much they improve the overall quality of your being, as well as the quality of your relationships. Then, share the victories with your friends and family; you just may improve their lives too!

THE HEADACHE ADVANTAGE FOR LIFE

Welcome to a whole new headache-free world. If you're not there yet, you will be soon. There's never been a better time to take self-care seriously and use the tools at your disposal to ensure your health. May the ideas in this book now be among your tools to prevent future pain. And in the event of an encounter with pain, you now have strategies to remedy it. I encourage you to visit my website at HeadacheAdvantage.com to access updates and additional resources and share your stories.

When I lecture and teach my "formula" to other healthcare practitioners, including medical doctors, they express gratitude for this knowledge and wish their formal training had included this perspective on pain patterns and headaches. Truth be told, it can take a very long time for curricula to change, even when new science emerges to change or modify previous information and advice. In fact, one of the motivating forces to write this book has been to help fill in this gaping hole. I hope that my voice and message can stimulate new research, start new conversations, accelerate the progress made in medicine and healthcare circles, and ultimately change the culture.

Readers like you are now empowered to spread the word and pass along this information. Imagine being able to help a dear friend or family member end a lifelong battle with chronic headaches.

My patients teach me every day. Some have suffered mightily for a long time and see me as their last resort. It amazes me what people will put up with for years or even decades before finding solutions to their pain, including pain that's emotionally rooted. We humans are an interesting species. We'll tolerate a lot before asking for help, rethinking old habits that don't serve us anymore, and opening our minds up to a different viewpoint. We may be programmed for pain, but pain is not *indefinitely* programmed into us. Don't accept pain as an inevitable fact of life. Pain is merely a messenger and teacher. Take *advantage* of it. For life! My hope is that you can now say goodbye to the old you and welcome a new you. And look for those opportunities for growth.

As I was putting the finishing touches on this manuscript, my mother Sue went through the final stage of her life over the holidays in 2023. She peacefully passed away in January. Watching her as she rapidly declined and eventually slipped away only strengthened my resolve to finish the book and get it into the hands of as many people as possible. The grief process taught me a lot, and among its lessons has been the paradoxical beauty of sadness and loss. They are indeed forms of pain, but they too can be incredibly inspiring and speak to what we should prioritize in the prime of our lives. The loss helped me to deeply ponder how the legacy of her life can now have meaning to transform and improve the lives of others. *I believe we are blessed with pain to elicit change.* Reflect on the growth you gained from a trial. Consider the character-building virtually every biblical character went through. We're designed to prosper in our pursuits, including those related to health and how we feel.

Now go thrive. And live life to your fullest potential.

Blessings,

Dr. V.

NOTES

The notes that follow offer a partial list of scientific papers, online destinations, and other references that you might find helpful if you want to learn more about some of the ideas and concepts expressed in this book. I've organized these notes chapter by chapter. Studies specifically referenced in the book are cited here. My hope is that these notes further lead you to places where you can inform yourself and discover new wisdom relevant to you and your health journey. Don't forget to visit HeadacheAdvantage.com for continual updates and a library of resources!

Introduction

1. Moheb Costandi, "Medication Overuse Headache a Pain to Treat," *Medscape Medical News*, December 7, 2023.
2. Luoping Zhang, et al., "Exposure to Glyphosate-based Herbicides and Risk for Non-Hodgkin Lymphoma: A Meta-analysis and Supporting Evidence," *Mutation Research/Reviews in Mutation Research* 781 (2019): 186–206. Also see: M. J. Davoren and R. H. Schiestl, "Glyphosate-based Herbicides and Cancer Risk: A Post-IARC Decision Review of Potential Mechanisms, Policy and Avenues of Research," *Carcinogenesis* 39 no. 10 (October 2018): 1207–1215.

Chapter 1

1. Timothy J. Steiner, et al., "Migraine Is First Cause of Disability in Under 50s: Will Health Politicians Now Take Notice?" *Journal of Headache Pain* 19, no. 17 (2018).

2. See: https://www.nih.gov/about-nih/what-we-do/budget

3. Jill Brook Hervik, Eva B. Foss, and Trine Stub, "Living with Chronic Headaches: A Qualitative Study from an Outpatient Pain Clinic in Norway, *EXPLORE* 19, no. 5 (2023): 702–709.

4. Joana Araújo, Jianwen Cai, and June Stevens, "Prevalence of Optimal Metabolic Health in American Adults: National Health and Nutrition Examination Survey 2009–2016," *Metabolic Syndrome and Related Disorders* 17, no. 1 (February 2019): 46–52.

5. For facts and statistics about diabetes, see: Diabetes.org and CDC.gov.

6. See the CDC's landing page that covers the facts of chronic diseases: https://www.cdc.gov/chronicdisease/index.htm.

7. N. Conrad, et al., "Incidence, Prevalence, and Co-occurrence of Autoimmune Disorders Over Time and by Age, Sex, and Socioeconomic Status: A Population-based Cohort Study of 22 Million Individuals in the UK," *Lancet* 401, no. 10391 (June 2023): 1878–1890.

8. For more about Dr. Chris Motley, see: DoctorMotley.com. Also see Dr. Motley's guest appearance on Josh Axe's "Ancient Health" podcast, episode 260: "How Our Thoughts Impact Our Physical Health" on January 19, 2024.

9. See the entry about "referred pain" at the Cleveland Clinic: https://my.clevelandclinic.org/health/symptoms/25238-referred-pain.

Chapter 2

1. G. Gilam, et al., "What Is the Relationship between Pain and Emotion? Bridging Constructs and Communities," Neuron 107, no. 1 (July 2020): 17–21

2. Y. Lin Y, et al., "Chronic Pain Precedes Disrupted Eating Behavior in Low-back Pain Patients," PLoS ONE 17, no. 2 (2022): e0263527.

3. E. Fuchs E and G. Flügge, "Adult Neuroplasticity: More than 40 Years of Research," *Neural Plasticity* (2014): 541870. Also see: M. Puderbaugh, and P.D. Emmady, "Neuroplasticity." In: StatPearls [Internet]. Treasure Island (FL): StatPearls Publishing. Available from: https://www.ncbi.nlm.nih.gov/books/NBK557811/.

4. Q. Su, et al., "Brain Regions Preferentially Responding to Transient and Iso-intense Painful or Tactile Stimuli," *Neuroimage* 192 (May 2019): 52–65.

5. Howard Schubiner, et al., "Application of a Clinical Approach to Diagnosing Primary Pain: Prevalence and Correlates of Primary Back and Neck Pain in a Community Physiatry Clinic," *The Journal of Pain* 25, no. 3 (2024): 672–681.

6. J. Sheng, et al., "The Link between Depression and Chronic Pain: Neural Mechanisms in the Brain," *Neural Plasticity* (2017): 9724371. Also see: Uri Nitzan, et al., "Initial Evaluation of Pain Intensity Among Depressed Patients as a Possible Mediator Between Depression and Pain Complaints," *Front Psychiatry* 10 (February 2019): 48.

7. A. J. Vickers, et al., "Acupuncture Trialists' Collaboration. Acupuncture for Chronic Pain: Update of an Individual Patient Data Meta-Analysis," *Journal of Pain* 19, no. 5 (May 2018): 455–474.

8. C. Zheng and T. Zhou, "Effect of Acupuncture on Pain, Fatigue, Sleep, Physical Function, Stiffness, Well-Being, and Safety in Fibromyalgia: A Systematic Review and Meta-Analysis," *J Pain Res* 15 (February 2022): 315–329. Also see: A. Xiang, et al., "The Immediate Analgesic Effect of Acupuncture for Pain: A Systematic Review and Meta-Analysis," *Evid Based Complement Alternat Med* (2017): 3837194.

9. R. E. Harris, et al., "Traditional Chinese Acupuncture and Placebo (Sham) Acupuncture Are Differentiated by Their Effects on Mu-opioid Receptors (MORs)," *Neuroimage* 47 no. 3 (September 2009): 1077–85.

10. F. Gómez-Pinilla, "Brain Foods: The Effects of Nutrients on brain function. Nat Rev Neurosci. 2008 Jul;9(7): 568–78.

11. Eva Selhub, "Nutritional Psychiatry: Your Brain on Food," Harvard Health Blog, September 18, 2022, https://www.health.harvard.edu/blog/nutritional-psychiatry-your-brain-on-food-201511168626.

Chapter 3

1. See EPA.gov.

2. Ibid.

3. For facts and historical data about diabetes and other metabolic issues, refer to CDC.gov.

4. L. Ricciuto, et al., "Sources of Added Sugars Intake Among the U.S. Population: Analysis by Selected Sociodemographic Factors Using the National Health

and Nutrition Examination Survey 2011–18," *Front Nutr* 8 (June 2021): 687643. Also refer to CDC.gov, namely: https://www.cdc.gov/nutrition/data-statistics/sugar-sweetened-beverages-intake.html.

5.   Z. S. Morris, S. Wooding S, and J. Grant," The Answer Is 17 Years, What Is the Question: Understanding Time Lags in Translational Research," *J R Soc Med* 104, no. 12 (December 2011): 510–20.

6.   C. E. Kearns, L. A. Schmidt, and S. A. Glantz, "Sugar Industry and Coronary Heart Disease Research: A Historical Analysis of Internal Industry Documents," *JAMA Intern Med* 176, no. 11 (2016): 1680–1685. Also see: Camila Domonoske, "50 Years Ago, Sugar Industry Quietly Paid Scientists To Point Blame At Fat," NPR.org, September 13, 2016; https://www.npr.org/sections/thetwo-way/2016/09/13/493739074/50-years-ago-sugar-industry-quietly-paid-scientists-to-point-blame-at-fat.

7.   R. B. McGandy, D. M. Hegsted, and F. J. Stare, "Dietary Fats, Carbohydrates and Atherosclerotic Vascular Disease," *N Engl J Med* 277, no. 5 (August 1967): 242–7 concl.

8.   H. Liu, Q. Wang, Z. Dong, and S. Yu, "Dietary Zinc Intake and Migraine in Adults: A Cross-sectional Analysis of the National Health and Nutrition Examination Survey 1999–2004," Headache 63, no. 1 (January 2023): 127–135.

9.   S. A. Read, S. Obeid, C. Ahlenstiel, and G. Ahlenstiel, "The Role of Zinc in Antiviral Immunity," *Adv Nutr* 10, no. 4 (July 2019): 696–710.

10.   R. H. Kwok, "Chinese Restaurant Syndrome," *New England Journal of Medicine* 278 (April 1968): 796.

11. For data and facts on glyphosate and other pesticides, see the National Pesticide Information Center at http://npic.orst.edu/.

12. P. J. Mills, et al., "Excretion of the Herbicide Glyphosate in Older Adults Between 1993 and 2016," *JAMA* 318, no. 16 (2017): 1610–1611.

13. L. Nummenmaa, et al., "Bodily Maps of Emotions," *Proc Natl Acad Sci* U S A 111, no. 2 (January 2014): 646–51.

Chapter 4

1. Dr. Robert Blaich, *Your Inner Pharmacy: Taking Back Our Wellness* (New York: Atria, 2006).

Chapter 5

1. A. Samsel, and S. Seneff, "Glyphosate, Pathways to Modern Diseases III: Manganese, Neurological Diseases, and Associated Pathologies," Surg Neurol Int 6 (March 2015): 45.

2. M. Zamani, et al., "Association Between Anxiety/Depression and Gastroesophageal Reflux: A Systematic Review and Meta-Analysis," *The American Journal of Gastroenterology* 118, no. 12 (December 2023): 2133–2143.

3. S. C. Dulawa and D. S. Janowsky, "Cholinergic Regulation of Mood: From Basic and Clinical Studies to Emerging Therapeutics," *Mol Psychiatry* 24, no. 5 (May 2019): 694–709.

4. Harvard Medical School. "Bile acids may help regulate gut immunity and inflammation." ScienceDaily. ScienceDaily, 3 January 2020. <www.sciencedaily.com/releases/2020/01/200103141047.htm>.

Chapter 6

1. See the American Thyroid Association: https://www.thyroid.org/

Chapter 7

1. S. K. Wood, and R. J. Valentino, "The Brain Norepinephrine System, Stress and Cardiovascular Vulnerability," *Neurosci Biobehav Rev* 74, Pt. B (March 2017): 393–400. Also see: X. Zhai, et al., "Noradrenergic Modulation of Stress Resilience," *Pharmacol Res* 187 (January 2023): 106598.
2. For a review of the gut-brain axis, see: J. Appleton, "The Gut-Brain Axis: Influence of Microbiota on Mood and Mental Health," *Integr Med* (Encinitas) 17, no. 4 (August 2018): 28–32.
3. M. Lyte, J. J. Varcoe, and M. T. Bailey, "Anxiogenic Effect of Subclinical Bacterial Infection in Mice in the Absence of Overt Immune Activation," *Physiol Behav* 65, no. 1 (August 1998): 63–8.
4. Martin J. Blaser, *Missing Microbes: How the Overuse of Antibiotics Is Fueling Our Modern Plagues* (New York: Henry Holt, 2014).
5. Rosebury T. Microorganisms Indigenous to Man. New York: McGraw Hill; 1962. Also see: Institute of Medicine (US) Forum on Microbial Threats. Ending the War Metaphor: The Changing Agenda for Unraveling the Host-Microbe Relationship: Workshop Summary. Washington (DC): National Academies Press (US); 2006. 3, The Ecology of Pathogenesis. Available from: https://www.ncbi.nlm.nih.gov/books/NBK57068/.

6. Emeran Mayer, *The Mind-gut Connection: How the Hidden Conversation Within Our Bodies Impacts Our Mood, Our Choices, and Our Overall Health* (New York: Harper, 2016).

Chapter 8

1. For a general overview about the pituitary, see the Cleveland Clinic's entry: https://my.clevelandclinic.org/health/body/21459-pituitary-gland

Chapter 9

1. For a general explanation of methylation, see the NIH's entry at: https://www.genome.gov/genetics-glossary/Methylation.
2. For a review of endocrine-disrupting chemicals (EDCs), see the entry at the National Institute of Environmental Health Sciences: https://www.niehs.nih.gov/.

Chapter 10

1. GBD 2021 Low Back Pain Collaborators, "Global, Regional, and National Burden of Low Back Pain, 1990–2020, Its Attributable Risk Factors, and Projections to 2050: A Systematic Analysis of the Global Burden of Disease Study 2021," *Lancet Rheumatol* 5, no. 6 (May 2023): e316–e329. Also see the American Association of Neurological Surgeons: https://www.aans.org/en/Patients/Neurosurgical-Conditions-and-Treatments/Low-Back-Pain.

Chapter 11

1. S. H. Chang, and Y. Choi, "Gut Dysbiosis in Autoimmune Diseases: Association with Mortality," *Front Cell Infect Microbiol* 13 (March 2023): 1157918.
2. M. A. Petrilli, et al., "The Emerging Role for Zinc in Depression and Psychosis," *Front Pharmacol* 8 (June 2017): 414.
3. Hossein Ebrahimi, et al., "A Randomized Clinical Trial of the Effect of Zinc Supplement on Depression and Anxiety in the Elderly," The Open Public Health Journal 14, no. 1: 537–544.
4. M. Evans, et al., "A Whole-Food-Based Health Product (A-F Betafood®) Improves Gallbladder Function in Humans at Risk of Gallbladder Insufficiency: A Randomized, Placebo-Controlled Clinical Trial," *Nutrients* 12, no. 2 (February 2020): 540.
5. A. Hatch-McChesney, and H. R. Lieberman, "Iodine and Iodine Deficiency: A Comprehensive Review of a Re-Emerging Issue," Nutrients 14, kno. 17 (August 2022): 3474.
6. See the Cleveland Clinic's entry on adaptogens: https://my.clevelandclinic.org/health/drugs/22361-adaptogens.
7. See the NIH's entry for magnesium in its "Dietary Supplement Fact Sheets": https://ods.od.nih.gov/.
8. L. Ferrara, "Nutrition and Phytotherapy: A Winning Combination Against Headache," *Int J Med Rev* 6, no. 1 (2019): 6–13.
9. See the NIH's entry for manganese in its "Dietary Supplement Fact Sheets": https://ods.od.nih.gov/.
10. See Mount Sinai's entry for manganese in its Health Library: www.mountsinai.org/health-library/.

11. M. Halland M, et al., "A Case-control Study of Childhood Trauma in the Development of Irritable Bowel Syndrome," *Neurogastroenterol Motil* 26, no. 7 (July 2014): 990–8.

Chapter 12

1. J. Fagan, L. Bohlen, S. Patton, and K. Klein, "Organic Diet Intervention Significantly Reduces Urinary Glyphosate Levels in U.S. Children and Adults," *Environ Res* 189 (October 2020): 109898.

2. V. Worthington, "Nutritional Quality of Organic Versus Conventional Fruits, Vegetables, and Grains," J Altern Complement Med 7, no. 2 (April 2001): 161–73.

3. D. Średnicka-Tober, et al., "Higher PUFA and n-3 PUFA, Conjugated Linoleic Acid, α-tocopherol and Iron, but Lower Iodine and Selenium Concentrations in Organic Milk: A Systematic Literature Review and Meta- and Redundancy Analyses," *Br J Nutr* 115, no. 6 (March 2016): 1043–60. Also see: C. M. Benbrook, et al., "Organic Production Enhances Milk Nutritional Quality by Shifting Fatty Acid Composition: A United States–wide, 18-month Study," *PLoS One* 8, no 12 (December 2013): e82429. Also see: M. Barański, et al., "Higher Antioxidant and Lower Cadmium Concentrations and Lower Incidence of Pesticide Residues in Organically Grown Crops: A Systematic Literature Review and Meta-analyses," *Br J Nutr* 112, no. 5 (September 2014): 794–811.

4. C. Ma, et al., "Association Between Bowel Movement Pattern and Cognitive Function: Prospective Cohort Study and a Metagenomic Analysis of the Gut Microbiome," *Neurology* 101, no. 20 (November 2023): e2014–e2025.

5. Peter J. D'Adamo, *Eat Right for Your Type: The Individualized Blood Type Diet® Solution* (New York: Berkley, updated edition, 2016).

6. Also see Dr. D'Adamo's site: https://www.dadamo.com/

7. J. Zhang, et al., "Identification of Poly(ethylene terephthalate) Nanoplastics in Commercially Bottled Drinking Water Using Surface-Enhanced Raman Spectroscopy," *Environ Sci Technol* 57, no. 22 (June 2023): 8365–8372.

Chapter 13

1. Dan Witters, "In U.S., Physical Health Plummets After the Pandemic," Gallup News, December 14, 2023: https://news.gallup.com/poll/546989/physical-health-plummets-pandemic.aspx.

2. Patrisha Antonaros, "Quarter of Americans Stressed 'All the Time'—But Cooking Might Be Key to Calm," StudyFinds.org, December 14, 2023: https://studyfinds.org/americans-stress-cooking-food/.

3. M. G. Kutlu, et al., "Dopamine Release in the Nucleus Accumbens Core Signals Perceived Saliency," *Curr Biol* 31, no. 21 (November 2021): 4748–4761.e8.

4. For a deep dive into the world of sleep medicine, see: Matthew Walker, *Why We Sleep: Unlocking the Power of Sleep and Dreams* (New York: Scriber, 2017).

5. N. Owen, et al., "Too Much Sitting: The Population Health Science of Sedentary Behavior," *Exerc Sport Sci Rev* 38, no. 3 (July 2010): 105–13.

6. S. Blacher, "Emotional Freedom Technique (EFT): Tap to Relieve Stress and Burnout," *J Interprof Educ Pract* 30 (March 2023): 100599.

7. Nenden Lesmana Wati, et al., "The Effect of EFT (Emotional Freedom Technique) to the Self Esteem among Nurses," *Malaysian Journal of Medicine and Health Sciences* 18, Supp2 (January 2022): 239–242.

ACKNOWLEDGMENTS

J esus changed my life. I was self-righteous and thought I had it all figured out. Broken and hurt, not able to share my passion for helping others, I decided to "try church" instead of my bike ride one fateful Sunday morning. That was soon followed by a retreat and answered prayer. No white dove, no parted sea, just a transformed life with even more zeal to heal others.

My wonderful wife of 32 years and three amazing daughters (and son-in-law) give me a reason to produce, to come home, to be present. Kim makes things happen. Kylie and Cole are beautiful souls. Alora is caring and faithful. Josi is persistence personified. These five beauties make my world a better place.

There have been many mentors in my life and, therefore, behind this book.

Kristin Loberg so patiently took the chaotic, choppy manuscript I had produced and made it come to life. She captured the desired tone and put it all together in an understandable, relatable project that now makes sense. Our weekly calls were powerful and productive because she is a rock star. I am so very thankful for our journey together.

Dr. Robert Blake was my first Applied Kinesiology teacher. His caring passion to mentor me and hundreds of others has dramatically shaped the way I view healthcare. I was fortunate to have served with him for over ten years early in my teaching career.

Dr. Scott Walker taught me how to release emotional triggers through the fine Neuro Emotional Technique on my 30th birthday. He has been a valuable mentor in so many ways ever since. He has worked tirelessly to appropriately document the effectiveness of emotional work through the ONE Research Foundation (https://www.oneresearchfoundation.org/).

The late Drs. George Goodheart (founder of Applied Kinesiology) and Wally Schmit (Quintessential Applications) were invaluable in enhancing my critical thinking while making physiology come to life.

Dustin Strong (StrongonHealth.com) has been a great sounding board. Our regular "shop talk," diving into physiologic nuances of neurotransmitters and other exotic biochemistry, helps keep it fresh and exciting. He's even stepped it up with our monthly Mastermind group calls.

There are numerous doctors/authors who have influenced my thinking, most of whom I have not yet met. Dr. David Perlmutter, Lee Carroll BSc, BHSc (WHM) MNHAA, Dr. Daniel Amen, Dr. Datis Kharrazian, Dr. Josh Axe, Dave Asprey, Dr. William J. Walsh, Kathleen McAuliffe, Martin J. Blaser, Emeran Mayer, MD, and Robert Lustig, to name just a few of a very long list. Most of their work I have read or listened to multiple times. *Keep learning, it inspires passion!*

Dr. Blake always concluded his 100-hour seminar series with the story of the traveler: The traveler was walking to the next town. He stopped and asked the farmer, "How long will it take me to get to the next town?" No answer. "How long will it take me to get to the next town?" No answer. So, the traveler began to walk. Then the farmer finally answered, "Two days." The frustrated traveler asked, "Why didn't you answer the first two times I asked?" Farmer: "Because I did not know how fast you were walking."

May we all walk fast and consistently. The number of true influences in my life is endless. I read the Bible daily. I listen to podcasts while in the car. I read books, blogs, and research papers when not treating patients. I teach others, which helps me learn. I listen to audiobooks while exercising. I truly try to make every minute bring value to me and, more importantly, to others. Keep growing and inspiring others.

Go to HeadacheAdvantage.com to find food and supplement protocols to continue your journey to vitality.

https://www.instagram.com/dr.vrzal/

https://www.facebook.com/Dr.Scott.j.Vrzal

I appreciate your motivation. You have now learned and implemented some key lifestyle changes. You now understand that:

Pain is intended to elicit *change*.
You are not a victim.
You are designed to THRIVE.

The advantage of pain in the head is that it can direct you to where your body needs help.

The advantage of reviews is that they direct people to trust a product.

Please take 60 seconds to click on a link below to leave an honest review of *The Headache Advantage* so that others will have the confidence to embrace this material.

Amazon/TheHeadacheAdvantage
Good Reads/TheHeadacheAdvantage

Thank you for taking the time share your valuable thoughts

INDEX

Acetylcholine, 58-60, 137
    tomatoes effect on, 63
Acid-blocking medications, 51, 117
Acupuncture, 14, 22, 47, 94
    reaction on opioid, 23
    Sham, 22
Adrenal glandular, 132
Air, 158
Antacids, 117
Anterior pituitary, 132
Anti-Yeast Supplement, 53
Anxiety, 59, 81, 162
    zinc deficiency link to, 119
Ashwagandha, 129
Aspartame, 148
Autoimmune Conditions, 51, 117
Autoimmunity, 152
Ayurvedic medicine, 129
Back Pain, Lower, 101-102
Bad Breath, 49, 82
Beets, 120-121
Berberine, 135
Beriberi, 50 *see also* Thiamine deficiency disease
Bile Production, 39, 58, 105, 120
Blaich, Robert, 47

Blood sugar, 96, 103-104
    probiotics use for, 139
Blood Type Diet, 151 see also immune type diet
brain's plastic powers see neuroplasticity
bread, 63, 145-146
Calcium, 51, 117-118
Chaste tree, 134
Chinese medicine, 11, 162
Chinese Restaurant Syndrome, 37
Chlorella, 140
Cholesterol, 56-57, high, 122, 133
Chromium, 135
Chronic constipation, 150
Chronic stress, 75, 77, 83
Circulation sex, 94
Circulatory System, 11, 78
Clean garden, 159
Coffee, 109
Colon, 102, 106
    congestion, 102
    glyphosate effect on, 139
    headband pain and, 138
    issues, 141
    problems, 105
    role, 107
Corn, 90, 96, 140

Cortisol, 45-46, 88-89, 129
Craig, Gary, 174
Craniosacral therapy, 114
Depression, 36, 59, 79, 81
Diabetes, 8, 104, 132, 149
    high rate of, 161
    sugar consumption on, 129
Diet, 27, 90, 142
    American, 29, 132, 149
    blood type, 151
    elimination, 140
    low-fat, 62
    meat-free, 154
    products, 146-147
Dietary cholesterol, 57
dietary fat, 56
    deficiency 122
    toxins, 55
    triggers, 26
Eastern medicine, 12, 48, 162
Eleuthero, 137
Elimination diet, 140
Emotional Freedom Technique (EFT), 174
Emotional health, 163
Emotional trauma, 141, 172
Emotional triggers, 26
Emotional villains, 40
Endocrine Disrupting Chemicals (EDCs), 98
Environmental chemicals see xenobiotics
Environmental insult, 38
Environmental triggers, 26
Eustress, 161
Exercise, 83, 155, 161
    buddy, 169
    snacks, 170

Fat metabolism, 56, 60, 135
Feet, 157
Fluoride, 124-126
Food, 24
Food-mood connection, 24
GABA (gamma-aminobutyric acid), 80, 107
Gallbladder, 54, 60
    congestion, 39
    glyphosate impact, 40, 58
    meridian, 24, 57 -58
    parasite and , 63
    tomatoes effect on, 63, 123
    treat the, 120-121
Gastroesophageal Reflux Disease (GERD), 59
Gastrointestinal (GI) Tract, 25, 34, 77-78
Glyphosate, 38-40, 90, 146
    on bile production, 58, 122
Goodheart, George, 47-48, 57
Gut, 25, 34, 79, 141
    dysbiosis, 117
    dysfunction, 81, 85, 141
    happiness starts in, 80
    infections, 84
    microbes, 79, 84
    permeability, 49
Gymnema, 135
H.E.A.D. protocol, 114
Hands, 157
Heachaches, 4
    back-Head Pain, 65
    Cyclops Headaches, 86, 90, 131
    Frontal (Forehead) Headaches, 75, 128

Left-Sided Headaches, 116

Pain In The Sides Of The Head (Temples), 92, 133

Pain That Surrounds the Head, 100, 138

Right-Sided Headaches, 54, 58

Triggers, 74

Heavy metal, 95, 125

Helicobacter pylori (*H. pylori*), 82-83, 118

HEPA air purifiers, 158

High blood sugar, 96

homeostasis, 164

Hormonal changes, 7

and dehydration, 35, 105, 139

Balance, 92, 161, 169

effect of stress, 99,

HPA axis, 89

hydrochloric acid, 51-52, 17

in supplement, 117

see also stomach acid

*Hyper*thyroidism, 68, 71, 126-127

Hypothalamus, 87-88, 166

Hypothyroidism, 66-67, 125

Ileal brake, 56

Immune system, 49, 51, 152-153

effect of stress on, 161

gallbaddder and, 60

reaction to irritant, 72, 105

sugar effect on, 103

Immune type diet, *see* blood type diet

Inflammation, 24, 28, 77, 106

systemic, 30, 82

Intestinal permeability, 34, 77

Iodine, 124-127

deficiency, 126

Irritable Bowel Syndrome (IBS), 141

IT band syndrome, 104

JAMA Internal Medicine, 29

Jensen, Bernard, 102

Knee, 57, 139

Large Intestine, 100, 102, 162

leaky gut, 34-35, 103

Lectins, 153

lifestyle, 9, 42

diet 149

effect on colon. 105

triggers, 90

Liquid calories, 29

Liver detoxification, poor, 96-97

Liver, 14, 33, 63, 97-98

glyphosate impact, 39

Magnesium, 129-130

Manganese, 132

Mark Lyte, 81

Martin Blaser*, 83

Memorial Sloan Kettering Cancer Center, 22

Memory loss, 58

Mercury, 125-126

Meridians, 10

Methylation, 97, 136, 154

Microbes, 79-80, 148

Microbiome, 24, 39, 82-83

artificial sweetener effect on, 148

function 80

Milk thistle, 99, 136

Molecular mimicry, 72, 125, 152

Monosodium Glutamate (MSG), 10, 35-36

sources 36

Mosquito magnet, 72-73
MSG symptom complex *see* Chinese Restaurant Syndrome
MTHFR gene, 95
Myrrh, 130
Nanoplastics, 159
National Institutes of Health, 5, 12, 23, 63
Nervous system, 11, 22, 169
    sympathetic, 40
    central 78, 130, 162
    intestinal, 78
    parasympathetic, 41
    enteric, 80
    gut 80
NET, 173
neural pathways, 12, 181
Neuro-Emotional Technique (NET)
Neuroplasticity,20
Neurotransmitters, 22, 25, 77, 79, 119
Nociceptors, 12-13, 20
Noradrenaline, 77-80, 83-84
Norepinephrine *see* Noradrenaline
Nutritional psychiatry, 24
Omega-6s, *149*
Organ body clock, 48
Pain receptors, 12 *see also* nociceptors
Pain
    pathology of, 17
    perceptions of, 19
    science of, 16
Parasites, 63, 107-108
p-cresol, 39
Phantom Limb Syndrome, 18
Pituitary gland, 86, 88, 132
Pituitrophin PMG, 132

Polyunsaturated Fats Omega-3 Fatty Acids, 149
Popliteus muscle, 57
Prevention, 8, 49
Probiotic, 121, 139-140
Probiotics, 139-140
Psychological trauma, 141
Qi (energy), 10, 48
Quadratus lumborum muscles, 102
Reproductive glands, 98
Reproductive hormones, imbalances in, 96
Right buttock (piriformis muscle), 113
Saccharin, 148
Seafood, 31, 36
Second brain see gut
Selective Serotonin Reuptake Inhibitors (SSRIs), 79
sensory perception, 21
Serotonin, 25, 79-81
Set points, 19-20
Seventh sense, 24
Sinus, 108-109
Sinusitis, 108
skin, 157
Sleep apnea, 166-167
Sleep, 161, 164
    release emotional pain, 171
Spanish black radish, 130
Stomach acid,49, 117-118 low, 45, 49, 108
    medication effect on, 51
Stomach, 11, 45, 47
Stress reduction, 114, 161, 172
T3 hormone (thyroglobulin), 125
T4 (thyroxin), 126

Temporal arteritis, 16
Thiamine diphosphate, 51
Thiamine hydrochloride, 50
Thiamine triphosphate, 51
Thiamine
        alcohol-induced, 33
        deficiency, 33, 72
        herpes, 98
        mosquito and, 73
        thyroid dysfunction, 127
Thyroid, 65, 68-69, 124-126, 131
Tomatoes, 63, 123
Toxic metals, 50, 62, 106, 119
Toxic Substances Control Act of
1976, 27
Trans fats, 55, 62, 122, 147
Trigeminal neuralgia, 113
Trigger, 8
TSH (thyroid-stimulating
hormone), 88-89, 132
Vagus nerve, 13, 254, 80
Vegetables, 31, 121

cruciferous, 123
lack of, 139
organic, 52, 73, 106
seeded, 119
Viral infections, 31, 116
Vitamin B12 (cobalamin), 136
Vitamin B5 (pantothenic acid),
137
Vitamin B6 (pyridoxal-5-
phosphate, or P5P), 33, 136
Vitamins B1 (thiamine), 30, 50-
51, 71, 99
Walker, Scott, 173
Water, 158
Wheat consumption, 50, 58
Wild yam, 134
Xenobiotics, 39
Yeast overgrowth, 102-104
Yeast, 34
Zinc, 31-32
        deficiency, 31-32, 119
        effect of sugar on, 30

Made in the USA
Columbia, SC
28 October 2024

0ea94b2f-a9e3-40ed-9098-5032ce161bc0R01